Bridge of Fire

Bridge of Fire
Sales Secrets from the Super Successful

Luther Gabriel "Gabe" Biondo

Bridge of Fire: Sales Secrets from the Super Successful

© Copyright 2019 Luther Gabriel Biondo

All Rights Reserved. No part of this book may be reproduced, stored in a retrieval system, or transmitted, in any form of, by any means, electronic, mechanical, photocopying, recording, or otherwise, without the written prior permission of the authors.

ISBN-13: 978-0-578-49157-8

Editing by Michelle Mullins
Cover design by Luisito C. Pangilinan

Bridge of Fire, LLC
P.O. Box 170155
Austin, Texas
United States of America

bridgeoffire.com
bofbook.com

What's most striking about Gabe's personality is that his passion is not singular. He is one hell of a drummer, song writer, father, businessman, and most importantly, he is a friend. I have spent many years in the trenches with him taking down deals and creating long-lasting customer relationships. He can wear out a mobile phone like no other. He does this because he not only likes to communicate, but he knows that winning is a team sport. If done alone, how can he teach, share success, and multiply what works? I can tell you with certainty the process Gabe uses leads to ultimate success.

I remember many meetings in large boardrooms where we were grossly outgunned by the competition, but in the end, the connection Gabe created led us to success. Ultimately, it was Gabe's unwavering passion to win that had the customers saying, "You know what—we like this guy from Houston, and we believe he will deliver."

Said differently, he is a master of weaving in a genuine personal connection while keeping the goal front and center.

With that, take the time and read the best practices in this book. You will not be disappointed, and I am certain if you work them daily, you will find that getting to the top is a "logical next step."

—Trey McCall
Head of Global Sales
Software Security Firm

About the Author

Luther Gabriel "Gabe" Biondo started his sales career in 1994 as a mobile telecom technician, installing cellular phones in cars when you could not carry them in your back pocket and summon the information world.

A Vice President of Sales, Frank Graham, witnessed Gabe speaking with ease to an upset customer that worked at a prominent law firm in Houston, Texas. He was impressed with how Gabe walked the customer off the proverbial ledge of high pricing and got her to buy a phone and a plan. Frank proceeded to invite Gabe to lunch and afterwards asked that he join the sales force.

This is where his story began. Frank took a chance on a 21-year-old with no sales experience, very little college education, and placed him in sales where the nearest peer was twice his age. Gabe had to learn the ropes with little to no training.

Literally selling the Internet and other new cutting-edge tech devices, plans, and services, Gabe went on to be the #1 salesperson in the market and eventually the country. Gabe has sold everything from door-to-door coupons, cutting edge technology, to Fortune 100 organizations, closing billions of dollars in sales.

Over the past quarter century, and in each category, Gabe has built a successful sales career climbing to the top, staying there, and documenting it all along the way. Gabe has taught sales techniques, sales strategies, and the models covered in this book to thousands of salespeople. His simple, candid, loving, often emotional approach has left many baffled at the simplicity of what it takes to get to the top and stay there. His instruction, message, and methods on how to be a top salesperson will leave a lasting impression. He truly cares about moving sales folks from the middle of the pack to the top because he himself has had to cross his own **Bridge of Fire**.

Dedication

To my parents, Sal and Patsy Biondo, who showed what is was like to do hard work everyday. And begged that I never make a living having to do it. I love you!

—Luther Gabriel Biondo

Table of Contents

Introduction **17**

Chapter 1 - Mindset **21**
    Own Your Mindset 21
    Modeling 24
    A Lesson on Accountability 26
    Know What You Want First 28
    Be Kind to Yourself 29

Chapter 2 - Honesty **31**
    From the Mouths of Customers 31
    Common Themes 34
    Get it Done the Right Way 35
    Adapting 36
    Honesty is the Best Policy 38

Chapter 3 - Trust **41**
    Accelerate Trust 42
    Be a Professional 43
    Elevate the Experience 45
    Reverse Bad Situations 46
    Be Aware of the Bad Stuff 47
    Get to the Core 48
    Say What You Mean 49

Chapter 4 - Fear **51**
    Two Major Fears 51
    Common Fears in Salespeople 52
    You Are Not Alone 53
    Five Ways to Overcome Fear 54
    Usefulness of Fear 61

Chapter 5 - Prospect **63**
    The Right Prospect 64
    Labeling 64
    Measure Activity 65
    Communication 66
    The Tale of Two Stories 68

Meaure Customers 69
Practice 70
Find Ways to Connect 72

Chapter 6 - Keep Going 75
Where Are You? 76
Burn the Boats 78
Set the Right Goals 78
Look for Progress, Not Perfection 79
Forensic Feedback 80
Control the Controllables 82
Reward Yourself Because You Deserve It 83
Daily Practices Build Monthly Results 84

Chapter 7 - Let Go of the Ego 87
Ego is Expensive 89
Lessons Learned 91
God Complex 91
How to Eliminate the Ego 92
Give More to Get More 93
Confidence vs. Ego 94

Chapter 8 - Get a Jacket 97
Biggest Bridge of Fire 98
Treasure Your Mentors 99
Your Inner Belief 100
Winners vs. Losers 101

Bonus Materials - Be Your Best 105
Posture 106
Meeting Manners 107
Mirroring 109
The Follow-Up 110
Clarifying Questions and Transparency 112
Using a Team Correctly 114
Closing and Asking for the Business 115
Five LinkedIn Message Templates 117

"The mind is everything. What you think, you become."
—Buddha

"The pendulum of the mind alternates between sense and nonsense, not between right and wrong."
—Carl Jung

"What the mind of man can conceive and believe, it can achieve."
—Napoleon Hill

"Courage is not having the strength to go on; it is going on when you do not have the strength."
—Theodore Roosevelt

Foreword

Gabe and I have known each other since grade school. I've seen him grow and change over the decades and I am not surprised by what I read in *Bridge of Fire*. Every word of it is read with Gabe's approach to customer service, sales, and profitability. Sales as a profession is often viewed as difficult, dirty, and disreputable. Most people do not succeed simply because they do not plan well, lack mentors, and leaders that can truly guide them, and most importantly, they find themselves facing unpleasant truths about who they are.

Bridge of Fire creates important pathways for current or future salespeople to understand that learning, understanding, and implementing the fundamentals of service, client relations, and internal drive are the keys to being successful in sales. Gabe's examples and research show both a high level of quality and passion for the sales profession and sales professionals.

In my work as a consultant and speaker, the same principles that Gabe outlines in *Bridge of Fire* are things that I need to implement. His concepts are universal whether your sales efforts are internal or external. The world has plenty of salespeople and sales-related books. *Bridge of Fire*, however, provides well-written, insightful tips to making sales enjoyable and truly about solving problems and addressing needs.

I am honored to call Gabe a friend, an accomplished musician, and a sales professional and mentor that serves others. And now, I can call him an author who is truly making the world better with his passion and his words. Please enjoy the book, take notes, and know that your journey to excellence will always require you to cross bridges of fire.

—Dr. Nguyen "Tom" Griggs
Founder, Lead Connect Grow LLC
Consultant, Speaker & Author

Bridge of Fire

#BRIDGEOFFIRE

INTRODUCTION

You most likely have come across the Pareto principle in some area of your life. Better known as the 80/20 rule, the Pareto principle states that, for many events, roughly 80% of the effects come from 20% of the causes. [1]

This applies in business as well. Almost 80% of sales come from the top 20% of customers, and 80% of sales revenue comes from the top 20% of salespeople.

It is true and may be hard to believe, but if you are not a top salesperson you may be costing your organization more money than you are bringing in. That's right. You, the average salesperson, with your business cards, smart devices, phone, office space, travel, and meal expenses. You may be costing your company money just by being employed and you are costing them more than you are making them. This is a big problem and organizations need you to step up and be a better seller to close the gap.

To set the tone for this book, salespeople do three things.

We Talk, Type, and Drive

It is not HARD WORK. Shoveling asphalt in 110-degree heat is hard work. Shoveling snow in negative 6-degree weather is hard work. Selling is not back-breaking, nor does it take a physical toll on the body. We talk to people, type on our devices, and drive to meetings. You may be smart and well-educated on your product, an expert or even an evangelist, but if you are not at the **top** month after month, then you are not exercising your full sales potential, and this is costing your organization precious and valuable dollars.

Many would never approach a burning bridge and attempt to cross it. This book will show you how to cross that **Bridge of Fire** from an average salesperson into a Sales Superstar, and it will provide specific ways to get out of the bottom 80% and into the top 20% (and beyond).

Your Company Needs You to Do This

If you are a salesperson manager, director, president, or officer at a company that is failing in sales, this book will guide you and show you how to create a top-performing sales organization.

Returning to the Pareto principle, *Inc.com* cites:

> Only a fifth of salespeople almost always exceed quota on the average team, which means by definition that 80 percent sometimes or often do miss their quota.[2]

This book is designed to get, **you**, the average salesperson, to the top and keep you there. You can skip around, write notes, highlight your favorite passages, and do whatever it takes to get the concepts. But you must do the work. Know that it is you, the reader, that needs to become the doer. You must be the one that acts and the one who moves outside of your own comfort zone and the one who creates the *right* result.

Remove your "I have tried everything" mind and take these steps that get you where you want to be, which is at the top. Reading this book will invoke an emotional response deep in the core of your being. It will command you to stop being average and push you to finally do what it takes to get to the top.

CHAPTER 1

Mindset

"If you believe you can or if you believe you cannot, you are right either way!"
—Henry Ford

Own Your Mindset

Efficacy refers to the power it takes to produce an effect. It is that simple. Top sales reps have a high amount of efficacy. They possess a strong belief that they can produce a desired or intended result. Belief is the single most important step in this process. There is a reason it is #1 and will be reiterated throughout the book. This is a very strong first lesson on purpose. You purchased this book because you are in the middle (or lower) of the pack and want to finally get to the top.

Trust that it is not as hard as you think. There are no magical talents top salespeople possess, nor is it politics, account sets, territory, better leads, or any of that nonsense. The first thing you must do is understand what you want. You must believe you can get it even if you do not know how yet.

You own your reality and your stories and everything in-between. The same thing can happen to two different people and the reaction will be vastly different. Winners win, doers do, believers believe, losers lose, and so on. But how do you go from being a loser to a winner in a short period of time in sales? How do you achieve something that you have never accomplished before? It starts with your "what." What do you want? You must know **WHAT** you want even if you do not know **HOW** to get it. And it all comes down to one simple, very basic first step: belief.

Four-Minute Mile

There was a time when no one could run a mile in less than four minutes. It was impossible. Most people thought the four-minute mark was impossible to break. They thought the human body couldn't physically go that fast or that it would collapse under the pressure. You were crazy to even try.

Sir Roger Bannister was the first man to run a mile in under four minutes and did it in less than ideal conditions.

This is how it was written in the *New York Times*:

> LONDON. It was not a pleasant evening. The weather was blustery, and it had been raining on and off all day. As the hundred bells of Oxford made their various attempts at announcing 6 o'clock, fewer than 2,000 undergraduates had assembled to watch the proceedings on the athletic field in Iffley Road. The students wound their damp scarves around their necks and stared at the sodden running track.

There was little enthusiasm and no excitement. Yet, a few minutes later, the students went wild, spilling across the cinders, skidding onto the grass, shouting, jumping for joy, throwing their hats in the air. And, half an hour later, the word was around the world: a man had run a mile in under four minutes. The dream of the old Greek athletes 2,000 years ago had been realized, the unattainable attained, a physical frontier extended by a gawky, nervous youth of 25 named Roger Bannister. The date was May 6, 1954.[3]

Roger had a clear vision. He wanted to beat the four-minute mile. He really didn't know how he would do it, but the lesson is he started with his "what."

Roger Bannister proved everyone wrong by training in his own way, not much at all compared to his competitors, yet his fame was based on what he wanted to do and ultimately believing that he could do it.

As incredible as that was, it is not the best part of the story. The highlight of the story and the lesson learned here is that Roger Bannister only held the record for a mere forty-five days until someone else came behind him and bested his record.

"The dream of the old Greek athletes 2,000 years ago had been realized." And in less than two months, others realized it too. Once someone proved that it could be done, limited thinking was eradicated, paving the way for more people to achieve what was once thought of as impossible.

Take a moment to let this sink in deeply. Roger Bannister did something no man or woman was able to do. This wasn't magic but magical.

Since timing the distance of a mile with runners, no human was able to beat the four-minute mile. It was thought that the human body was physiologically incapable of this achieving this feat. Maybe it was due to too much wind resistance, too small of leg muscles, or not enough lung capacity. It was rumored that the Greek Olympians fed runners tiger milk as an effort to help them run faster and even had a tiger chase the runners to help them get past the four-minute mile.

It was *thought* that breaking the four-minute mile was impossible until Roger Bannister came along on a damp evening and mystified the entire running world. And then a month and a half later, someone else did it again.

The four-minute mile has since been broken by over 1,400 athletes and is now the standard of all professional middle-distance runners. In the 64 years since, the mile record has been lowered by almost 17 seconds, and the current stands at 3:43.13.

This is phenomenal and many of you can stop here, look around, see that what you are chasing is possible and go on with the belief that you can do it and ultimately get it done.

"If you change the way you look at things, the things you look at change."

—Wayne Dyer

Separate yourself from the 80% and get yourself into the top 20%. Believe you can do this. Close your eyes, take a deep breath, and visualize you being in the top 20%. If you cannot comfortably do this, go find some inspiration.

Modeling

Who is your Roger Bannister? Find that person in your organization that has the results you want and follow suit. Find a mentor and be a mentee to that person. If that person is not near you, then do it virtually. With today's technology, it is like you can be in the same room.

See and realize that it is possible to achieve and believe you can do it. Almost anyone who is successful most likely began simply with the belief that they could do it. Belief is not the only thing, but it is the first step to achieving the right results.

Change your thoughts, change your beliefs, and you will change your world!

Let's look at one woman who began a sales job because she needed more money and heard sales was the way to get it. She was a single mother and had three kids. Her customer service career was not going as planned, which had a huge impact on her financial life. She needed to be the best of the best. Her electricity was cut off when she first encountered the material in this book. She moved into a sales job and was failing miserably. She wanted to make enough money to never worry about getting her electricity turned off again but didn't know where to begin.

When starting her sales journey, she never made more than $45,000 a year. She was tired, anxious, and fearful that she was going to have to claim bankruptcy. These were desperate times and she knew that she needed to act fast.

She began by shifting her belief that making greater than $100,000 in sales was possible. Not only was it possible, but she could probably start in just a few days. There were a few examples in the office of people doing this and it dawned on her that they were not any more talented than she was. She thought, "If they can do this, I most certainly can!" and this was an important first lesson.

She followed the principles in this book and has not made less than six figures since. More importantly, she has never had her electricity turned off again. Currently, her W2 is north of $250,000 and growing.

She is a testament that this works, and many others have used these principles to make lots of money. Let's face it: if you are in sales and reading this book, it is most likely because you want to make lots of money. Sales is a for-profit profession that many get into because of the financial rewards, and you should expect to receive lots of rewards for doing the work.

Companies need passionate people to push their product, to sell their homes, technology, cars, fitness programs, office furniture – almost everything has a salesperson behind it!

A Lesson on Accountability

Take this quick five-question quiz to determine if you are an Action Taker or an Excuse Maker:

1. You only have a few contacts in an account or prospect list, and they will not respond to your communication efforts:

    A. Give up and say you will try again later—but never do.
    B. Provide an excuse on their behalf as to why they are not responding to make yourself feel better.
    C. Research sales tools such as LinkedIn, diversify personal contact lists, and find additional targets to contact.

2. Your meeting cancels and you have two hours before your next appointment:

    A. Yell, "Bagel break!" and check social media.
    B. Walk around the office or call your colleagues and disturb them with complaints about how meetings always cancel.
    C. Immediately reset the date for the cancelled meeting and use the extra time for prospecting.

3. Your sales activity is light on calls and meeting activity:

    A. Do nothing and hope that a customer or prospect will call you.
    B. Spend lots of time talking with your sales leader on why your customers may be sick, out on vacation, or just do not need to meet.
    C. Wake up early, get organized, find additional opportunities to meet, scrub the customer base. and get after it.

4. You missed your quota:

    A. Proclaim the unfairness of quotas, doing nothing about it, while discussing the latest news, sports scores, etc.
    B. Spend lots of time talking with your sales leader on why your customers are broke and have no budget, competition is too tough, not know why you lost your deals, and remain ignorant about your deals.
    C. Hit your quota based on your pre-emptive efforts to get to your goal.

5. You missed your quota again:

    A. Blame the tools, the processes, the people, the pay, and the customers.
    B. Cheer on the competency of the competition and why they are so much better (they are saying the same about you when they lose, by the way).
    C. Get determined to never lose again, make it a point to know why you lost, learn from it, and move forward with an action plan. Think that you can do it and then act like it.

Based on those answers, what did you learn? Do you make excuses or are you one who takes immediate action? If you are in the bottom percentile of sales, you are probably making excuses.

Who Wants to Be an Excuse Maker?

Now obviously the "C" answers are those who act, and the rest are making excuses. This is to demonstrate that common complaints from the average salesperson are the same.

Also, there is a reason I listed "missed your quota" twice. The goal is to get those that rarely succeed to a place where success is common, expected, and no Excuse Makers live.

Know What You Want First

Being an Excuse Maker may be a hard habit to break. Excuse Makers are looking for, focused on, and are used to finding excuses. This is a bad habitual pattern that has gone on for a long time. Excuse Makers have the reflex of finding the "not my fault" in everything.

Do you notice that when you buy a car, you suddenly see the same car almost everywhere you go? Is this because more of these cars are built? Or is it because you may have a heightened awareness or a more focused attention on that car? This is true when it comes to excuses versus actions. Are you looking for the excuse that keeps you from performing like a true Action Taker? Much like that car that you are focused on, they do not suddenly appear out of nowhere. It is simply that you are focused on the excuse, and boom—there it is!

Now apply that solution to winning. This exercise works on a cellular level. Do you realize how these steps are now starting to manifest together?

First, you must know winning exists and then look for it. Magically it appears. What you do not realize is it has been there the whole time. What's the difference now? How is it everywhere now?

You believe you can see something and then it comes into your life. I have a specific, white, German-made car and now I see them everywhere. I am sure there are red ones and blue ones and green ones, but I see the one that I have because my focus and awareness are on the color of the model I drive every day. This is called the Reticular Activating System (RAS). It is a bundle of nerves at our brainstem that filters out unnecessary information, so the important stuff gets through.

Here is a simple exercise: Look around and focus on brown. How much brown can you find? Now scan again and look for red. How much red did you find in the same area? Now, look for success. Look for the ability to win. Look for the solution and you will find it. Be careful because the same goes for the excuses.

Each time you do not achieve or receive a desired outcome, review and visualize what it would have looked like if you had won the opportunity or received your desired outcome. Was it right in front of your face?

Invest attention into your thoughts and see if blaming others or making excuses begin to arise. If this process starts, be patient and start over. Do this until you can accurately visualize what happened and begin to take accountability for the situation. This exercise will help when you are moving into situations and start to feel the blame game come up. Take hold of the situation and make it happen. And remember – when you lose all your excuses, you will find all your results! This is not easy and will require patience with yourself.

Be Kind to Yourself

It is estimated that we have over 50,000 thoughts per day. It is vitally important that you are kind to yourself and try to have positive thoughts. We talk to ourselves more than we talk to anyone else. So, BE KIND!

You are your only you and nothing good comes from negative self-talk. As we move through this journey to sales excellence, you want your best friend talking you through the tough times. So be your own best friend. Be kind to yourself. I cannot emphasize this enough. You will notice that the kinder you are to yourself, the easier the tough times are. You can control your thoughts and you will ultimately control your results. When the negative thoughts come up, be patient and replace them with positive thoughts and images of winning. Think of a time where you were able to achieve the seemingly unachievable and remember, that was you. So be kind and continue to allow yourself the space to grow into this new mindset. Do not beat yourself up if you did not score very well on the "Lesson on Accountability" exercise. Just realize that you took the step to get this book and that is showing you are taking responsibility for your own success.

Summary

- Get your mindset right by believing you can do this.
- Find your Roger Bannister or the person achieving the results you want and think, "If they can do this, so can I!"
- Own your accountability—know that being an Excuse Maker will never work.
- Focus on finding the wins, the success, and follow through with results.
- Be kind to yourself.
- What are you telling yourself?
- What are you believing to be true?
- What is the truth?

CHAPTER 2

Honesty

"No legacy is so rich as honesty."
—William Shakespeare

Honesty is the best policy and your customers deserve and require the truth. I have heard this time and time again and made it a point to drive this home from the mouths of actual customers. When preparing for this book, a poll was taken from various levels of customers ranging from Supply Chain Managers to Vice Presidents, to Fortune 100 companies, down to small and medium businesses. Below are a few of their responses.

Why is the quote, "Honesty is the best policy," important to you and why would you want your salesperson to abide by this policy?

From the Mouths of Customers

Leslie Daily, Fortune 100 Procurement

"As has been drilled into our heads, 'Honesty is always the best policy,' and that still rings true today. I have been a global buyer working with salespeople from the pool of diversity and cultural institutions and there are always two things I kept close to my core methodology of doing business.

First, 'Never put a good company out of business' – meaning your customers, vendors, or prospects also have to make a profit. To chase a dime over a dollar is burdensome and not in good faith. The second is honesty and I demanded it of my vendors. There has always been the notion that the salespeople are slick and cheesy, and you can spot one a mile away because you felt like you were being cheated. I know that when I meet a vendor for the first time, I mentioned the first core ideal of never put a good vendor out of business, but that I also required that same ethos from my vendors. It is easy to say that the more open and honest I felt my salesperson was, the more likely I was to happily accept pricing even if I knew I could get a better discount. Honesty puts reality on the table. There will be days that you give more than you should, but in return, by being honest you will make more and gain more long term in good will and efforts.

Longevity should be the goal of a salesperson over the quick and large sale; it may be a $1 million deal today, but $10 million over the lifetime of that relationship, and that speaks volumes on your skills as a devoted salesperson.

Additionally, it was easy to justify and influence procurement decisions with my leadership team. I had their backing to fire bad vendors for even the smallest dishonesty, but on the flip side it went further in the discussions if I could fight for their honesty in doing business with us. Honesty is so much richer in building the foundation of a strong relationship and that building a strong relationship on honesty will carry you through the mistakes, challenges, and the good days. Honesty will carry you beyond your current role and will be pivotal in bridging the changes and challenges of your career. Live it, love it, breathe it!"

John McFall, VP of IT, Billion-Dollar Medium-Sized Business

"For me, each sale is like entering a relationship with a new partner in life. Trust must be built, and this is earned, not given lightly. Over time, interaction by interaction, and later, deal by deal, a common ground is formed between the buyer and the seller. The buyer needs to know that the seller has their best interest at heart. Is the seller available for the midnight emergency that we all suffer from time to time? Does the seller react in a meaningful way when the buyer has a real need apart from that of an actual financial transaction?

If the seller is only in it for the almighty dollar, then this will show quickly. Do not get me wrong, this is part of the deal. No doubt that the seller is trying to put food on the table. But there is a right way and a wrong way to go about this and you must have a solid foundation based on trust and honesty. Both the buyer and the seller each gain something from each interaction, whether it is intellectual capital from the exchange of information or the purchase of goods or services. Being honest and forthright builds that trust and ultimate dependence, to some degree, on the knowledge and expertise of the seller.

I refer to the parties as the buyer and the seller but at the end of the day, it is more than that if the relationship is built on trust and honesty!"

Marcus Rhamming, Fortune 100 Supply Chain Director

"I need salespeople to be accountable and responsive, knowledgeable about their organization and their industry, and establish trust within both organizations. The only way for the engagement to work is if there is long-term mutual value. I can hardball you and make you lose money, and you can over-price me. I do not always have visibility into every aspect of the cost drivers for what I am asking for and I need to leverage trust to ensure that I am asking for their right solution.

Most of the time the business has a result in mind and is guessing at the products or services which bring that result into reality. But without a good salesperson we get what we ask for—not what we need in terms of a solution.

So, in terms of a category strategy, firing the sales team is about as effective, if not more effective, than firing the supplier. 'Good' is the ability to navigate the above to help achieve the goals of the organization the salesperson is serving."

Common Themes

This comes straight from the customers' mouths and minds. All customers know that salespeople and companies must make money. They acknowledge it and even invite the opportunity to do so when they find an honest salesperson. It may seem obvious, but salespeople already have a tough hill to climb because most are turned off by the typical "salesy salesperson." Being interested in what the customer needs means staying maniacally focused on achieving that, and delivering on it will show that you do what you say. Refer to the summary in chapter 1:

- What are you telling yourself?
- What are you believing to be true?
- What is the truth?

Sometimes we might utilize the "FITFO" model. If a customer asks if we can deliver X, Y, and Z, we will say yes even though we might not have done this before. We know it may be a challenge but that it can be done. Now it is time to "Figure it the F*** Out!" Conversely, if we say yes just to get the sale, but we do not know for certain that we can make it happen, we are jeopardizing our relationship with dishonesty. There is a difference between the two scenarios and it is important to understand the different ways to approach this to make certain you come out on the right side of it.

Get It Done the Right Way

Top salespeople utilize the FITFO model to deliver and execute. This greatly impresses customers and keeps them coming back, whereas other average salespeople say that it cannot be done, or they haven't seen it before and avoid trying to figure it out.

I have seen average salespeople *avoid* the FITFO model and this is a devastating thing to witness. An amazing opportunity comes across their path and because they do not know how to get it done, they will tell the customer that it cannot be done. And this is something that is not truthful and even a bit lazy. Never be afraid to point out that your product or company may not be the right fit, but do not give up because it may take extra work to make it a fit.

The Japanese have no exact words for yes and no. English speakers would likely mistake the words "はい" (hai) and "いいえ" (iie) as equivalents to "yes" and "no" respectively, but they actually signify agreement or disagreement. They generally use a wide range of expressions to avoid having to say a strong no. For example, they may say the word "chotto" to convey the "difficulty" in answering the request.

In your sales process, do not say: "It cannot be done." Doing so ends the conversation and therefore, the sales opportunity. You should not say that it *can* be done either, if you are unsure. Instead, highlight the parts of your solution that will meet the customer's requirements 100% and then state that, "...and we'll figure out how to address this one portion to make it work for you." Notice the use of the word "and" instead of "but." Using the word "but" will negate all of the positive elements of your solution. Using the word "and" gives you a way out just in case, for whatever reason, you are unable to resolve that one specific item with your product or service so that it will meet the customer's needs.

Adapting

Nature has put you together, so be and act as your natural self. It will pay off!

It is hard to fake who you are over long periods of time. Whether you are in transactional or relationship business, you cannot fake who you are for extended periods of time. You must be your authentic self. It is not a sustainable model of success to falsify yourself for the sale. The best and most successful salespeople are themselves. I know it sounds simple, but here are a few examples. If you are funny, be funny. If you like to tell stories, tell stories. If you are structured, be structured. If you have high mathematical and analytical skills, use that to your advantage, but be yourself. Make sure that your authentic self comes across. This is where average salespeople get it wrong. Average salespeople may avoid others with different skill sets or worse, become extremely judgmental, and will not approach customers or prospects that they cannot easily identify with.

While it is imperative to make sure you are your true self, be open to adapting. Adapting is to make something suitable for a new use or purpose, to modify, or in other words, to become adjusted to new conditions or situations.

Humans are thought to be the most adaptable species on the planet. Think about how we have had to adapt to different climates or terrains over time, such as migrating from one continent into another, or having had to adopt different tribes' behaviors and rituals in order to survive. This is built into our DNA. We are less challenged these days as we do not have to pick our own berries to eat and rarely must we hunt for our dinner, but you get the point.

"The secret to success is knowing where to fit in, and how to stand out. It is fundamental to making a contribution and having a real impact; it lies at the heart of your sense of belonging, as well as your ability to be distinctive and receive recognition and appreciation. Know your own way to fit in and stand out."
—Caroline Purkhardt, *Stillness in Action*

Stay in tune with your customers' likes and personalities. Adapting is realizing who your customer is and meeting them at that place in life.

This is not faking or mimicking your customer or betraying your natural self, nor is it changing your personality from the core of who you are. However, it does require you to understand your customer's personality traits and values. Daniel Goleman, author of a *New York Times* bestseller book titled *Emotional Intelligence*, highlighted the importance of these capabilities, namely self-awareness, self-regulation, and empathy. No one is expecting you to go on a hunting trip if you are an animal rights activist, but you might reserve your comments on your activism while in a professional setting. This is an extreme example, but it drives home the point.

Take time to get to know who you are meeting so you can plan. You want to create immediate comfort so to focus on the sales situation. This allows you to build the rapport which is a prerequisite for a strong relationship that will last past the first transaction.

Getting in rapport with your customer is the most important thing that you get to do.

Once you are face to face, pay attention to the smallest details. Mannerisms are important and if you adapt to the customers you are more likely to see them open and share more. Mirror their tempo, identify with how they act, and do your best to be adaptable and watch how far it gets you. More is covered on this in the bonus materials.

Honesty is the Best Policy

Honesty is the best policy when it comes to who you truly are and what you are truly doing. I know some lazy, delusional salespeople out there that are full of excuses yet truly believe that they are the best at what they do. Sales is an easy occupation to determine whether one is successful or not.

Are you outperforming your peers consistently? Are you outperforming your quota, your commitments, and hitting your upside month after month? If you are not, then do not lie to yourself and do not let excuses get in your way.

Be brutally honest with yourself. Are you lying to yourself? Are you truly doing all the work that it takes to be successful?

Self-awareness is a crucial component of success.

- Are you honestly waking up and starting the day off successfully?
- Are you honestly making as many calls as you possibly can?
- Are you honestly following up consistently and in a timely manner?
- Are you honestly practicing the positive self-talk to stay encouraged and energetic?

Or are you just faking it, going along, not really doing the work but telling everybody you are? Are you populating your CRM or just doing some of the surface work to create the impression that you are working, but not putting forth maximum effort?

The question is, are you being brutally honest with yourself? Not mean, but honest. Remember, be kind to yourself, but not deceptive. If you are deceiving yourself, you will need to start right now by truly reflecting on how to change the lack of effort. More importantly, you must always remain honest.

Wake up and start the day with intentions to succeed. Organize yourself in a way to make all the prospecting calls that you need to make, do all the follow-ups meaningfully, and create your own success.

Remember, we talk, we type, and we drive. And doing that consistently over extended periods of time throughout the day will get you the results you desire.

Being brutally honest about the activities you are doing, with the right mindset, is a key factor to becoming a successful salesperson.

Remember the Excuse Maker versus the Action Taker lesson. You are an Excuse Maker if you are making excuses about why you cannot do your job. Instead, take the necessary action to remove those excuses or obstacles to get it done. That's being honest with yourself.

Summary

- Honesty is the best policy—with your customers AND yourself.
- Apply the FITFO model and deliver for your customer.
- Always be honest with yourself in all ways.
- Do the right work, early and often.
- Once you lose all your excuses, you will find all your results.

CHAPTER 3

Trust

> "The best way to find out if you
> can trust somebody is to trust them."
> —Ernest Hemingway

Love and hate can be accelerated but trust cannot. We have reviewed being authentic, being yourself, and adapting to create immediate focus on the job at hand. We have demonstrated being honest with your customer and brutally honest with yourself. You are ready to be committed to doing the right work, early and often. We have learned the FITFO model and how to apply it correctly. Now let's move on to building trust.

If you are representing a product or service that is not an easy sell or you are hearing more no than yes, it is likely that the customer does not trust that you can deliver on what you are promising. Or they simply may not trust you.

Building trust is identifying your customer's specific need and delivering the exact product, service, or solution to which you have committed. It is usually that easy, but sometimes it's not.

Do you know your audience? Do you understand the customer's specific problem? Are you able to articulate that problem back to them concisely, both parties agreeing to what is being solved and how? Do they trust that you can do it? Are you trustworthy? Do you do what you say you are going to do? Or worse, do you say you, your product, or service can do something that you know cannot be done?

How do you earn the customer's trust? Love and hate can be accelerated, but trust must be earned over time. You can fall in love with someone in a short span of time (especially after a couple of drinks). And you can quickly hate somebody. But it is very rare that you will trust anyone immediately.

Accelerate Trust

If at any time you ask for a customer's trust by saying, "Trust me," you better damn well be trustworthy and do exactly what they need you to do. Customers will listen to what you say lightly but watch how you act heavily. Salespeople already have a stigma of saying things they cannot do. So, you have never taken on a large project for a customer or you have never transacted with them, but you want them to trust that you can handle the job. Simply put, words are not enough, but do help with the overall task of getting someone to trust you. Trust may be built quickly by consistently doing exactly what you say you will do in a short period. If you want people around you to value your relationship, you must truly believe that relationship-building is important. Healthy relationships are built on a foundation of trust.

How is trust accelerated? Be curious about people. Review their LinkedIn profiles, research their interests, alma maters, any groups they belong to, and invest time in getting to know what makes them uniquely THEM.

Seek out commonalities and have a real dialogue. People are drawn to those who show true interest in them. Curiosity about people is a crucial element of relationship-building and will accelerate your ability to build trust. Having an abiding fascination in others gives you the opportunity to learn new things and make new connections. Do not try to impress them with how interesting and well-traveled you are, but instead try and seek out how you might be impressed by them.

Do the mundane extraordinarily well and be consistent. If you meet someone for the first time and have their business address, send them a hand-written thank you. One of the best techniques to accelerate trust is in following up with them after meeting or doing business together.

Follow-up is critical because remembering to be responsive can significantly impact sales and the business. It makes everyone feel like their needs are being attended to and customers really appreciate it. More is covered on this in the bonus materials.

If you discuss a topic you are both fond of and you have materials that they may not have, tell them you will send it and do so immediately. That person will trust that you are listening and that you will do exactly what you say you are going to do. It is a relationship-building exercise, but it is also a trust-building exercise. Mention that you are going to do something and do it.

Seek the truth for your customers and they will appreciate it. Trust emerges when you approach selling as a way of helping the customer discover areas where you can truly work together.

Be a Professional

This simple, straightforward instruction seems obvious. But you would be surprised how often this is overlooked. Making inappropriate comments, discussing controversial topics, and bad-mouthing the competition or a competitive product shows bad form and certainly does not instill trust.

The secret weapon that successful salespeople use is trust. Once again, make sure you are doing what you say you are going to do. Sign up for some easy-to-do items to help accelerate the trust-building exercise. It is very simple. These types of things work. Some may think this is obvious. Of course, you plan to do what you say you are going to do. But there are a lot of salespeople out there who do not:

> I am going to send you this quote.
> I am going to send you that article.
> Hey, I noticed that book over there. I'll show you a similar one.
> I am going to send you an invite for this particular event.

...And then you never do it. The customer will remember and the next time you say you are going to do something, they are not going to trust that you are going to do it.

Statistics show 99% of customers buy from salespeople they trust, and trust is a firm belief in the reliability, truth, ability, or strength of someone's words or actions. Trust, like honesty, is a key component to having a successful sales career, so build a trusting relationship. What you say and do matters, and the customer must know that you are trustworthy. Successful salespeople are completely present when they talk to prospects and customers. They are not thinking about another deal, being distracted, or sending emails to their team members. They are engaged and as a result, their conversations are deeper and more meaningful.

Active listening may be one of the hardest skills to develop, since it is human nature to care more about what you must say than your customer or prospect. However, it is incredibly valuable to learn how to do so. Not only will you build stronger relationships, but you will unlock information that'll help you position your product or service as the best option.

Elevate the Experience

The best thing you can do to earn a customer's trust is to do more than what you say you are going to do. We live in a world where information is abundant, but time is not. If you are making the time to go above and beyond, it really sticks out. Make going above and beyond a habit. Consistently elevating the experience is one of my favorite things to do. It shows genuine interest in creating a positive experience and better yet, it increases trust.

It can be as easy as noticing the dry erase markers are not working and sending them a package of new ones with a hand-written note. Food is the way to everyone's heart. If your lunch meeting is cancelled due to a last-minute project, offer to bring them lunch. Delivering pizza to a customer who has missed an introductory call or meeting is a great way to elevate the experience.

Friday ice cream delivery is always popular. People are typically seated in cube farms these days, so showing up on a Friday after lunch with cartons of ice cream, cones, a scoop, and some napkins will go a long way. Walk the aisles, shake people's hands, smile, and offer them ice cream to get them talking about you in no time. That is the fun stuff.

Consultants Joel Maynes and Alex Rawson stated that:

> When establishing a link to value is done well, it provides a clear view of what matters to customers, where to focus, and how to keep the customer experience high on the list of strategic priorities.

When it comes to your product, show up if there is a technical demo being delivered. If you are in a quoting situation, create multiple options without the customer having to ask. These small gestures will go a long way and create a meaningful, trusting relationship. Use customer service to drive the customer experience. Every customer interaction with you is a chance to add value. Elevating the experience is critical for creating and retaining customers and gaining advocates. Proactively going above and beyond creates the belief that you will always do this. And you must. Building the habit of being trustworthy is exhausting if you are constantly doing and going above and beyond without reward. So be selective with what you say you will do, but do what you say you are going to do. Make mention of doing this and be clear with your intentions. This builds a trusting relationship. Trust works both ways. If you continuously say and do what you sign up for and the opposite is not true, you have earned the right to bring this up in a non-confrontational way. Remind the customer or prospect that you are sticking to your word. If you get the notion that they are only taking and not willing to give, you cannot trust that they will do what they say, and you can move on.

Reverse Bad Situations

If you are in a bad situation or have caused a bad situation, do not let it ruin your day and do not let it stop your efforts. If your promise didn't manifest, if your commitment fell through, or if you forgot something, attack it with honesty and commit to getting back to work. Do not avoid accountability, do not assess blame, do not dodge the situation, but tackle it head on.

If your product fails to deliver what was promised or if a bug or mistake took place, acknowledge the error and take responsibility for it:

> This is on us and I will work to make sure that this does not happen again.

If you are late to a call or meeting, apologize once and do not make excuses, or worse, explain why you are late. Nobody cares, it wastes time, and it will likely come off as a flimsy excuse.

If a shipment did not show up on time because you didn't place the order on time, be accountable and do what you can to make it right:

Trust is paramount in relationships and I know what this looks like. I will work to fix this and make sure this is not a permanent scar.

In a meeting where there is silence coming from the other end, be patient and try to engage. Rather than just lecture, set up what-if scenarios about business problems and invite your customer to fill in some of the blanks about how they have solved them.

Keep this light and do not make it too long in your overall meeting, but there is some genuine fun in trying to figure certain kinds of questions out. It can even be as simple as sketching out a business problem or situation on one slide or hopping up on a whiteboard and drawing out how you interpret their problems or scenarios. Ask for an educated guess what they envision the fix to be.

Be Aware of the Bad Stuff

Some customers may have the thought that you are unable to handle clear, direct feedback. If you have an idea that the conversation may be bad, stoke the conversation. Convey that they can trust that you are a professional and can handle feedback. Remind them some of the best relationships sometimes start off rocky. Often it is their job on the line to trust a new vendor or provider of a product or service. Being upfront right away with words affirming that a bad situation may have taken place is where you need to start. Make sure and ask the right questions to get to the right answers. You most likely will not find out what the exact problem is by being vague and asking, "How are things going?" You most likely will receive surface-level answers and they will confirm that they may need to move on.

Most importantly, reward the bearer of bad news. When clear feedback is delivered, make certain you acknowledge their communication immediately and with gratitude:

I know that may have been uncomfortable and for that I thank you. Without providing me that feedback, we could not have gotten to the core of the problem and for that I commend you.

This honest observation will help open them up and help you get to the core.

Get to the Core

Make sure you are inquisitive on what specifically the customer is needing, wanting, saying, implying, and so on. If you are not clear, take a moment and ask another question. Answering a question with a question is the best way to achieve clarity. Do not overuse this technique, however, as it may also distract the conversation. But use it judiciously to get a very clear understanding of what is needed to navigate the conversation.

Provide clear communication on what you need and want from the customer up front so there are no misunderstandings. Clear communication and expectations at the beginning will help keep both parties accountable and more importantly, build significant trust faster.

Clarifying questions should not go on forever because eventually you just seem needy. Listen to trigger statements and phrases that are vague. Behind these statements, however, you know there is something else. For example, if you hear, "Well, you know how it is," you can respond with, "I know how it is at other places, but how is it at your organization?"

If someone uses a term that seems to be generic, you can politely ask them to expand. They say, "We have the standard number of employees doing this." Your response is, "What is standard?" These are simple and the exercise is to get the customer at the core of their need. If they continue to talk to you, then you will have a better grasp of what they need, and you can help them more precisely, thus building more trust. This is the goal.

Say What You Mean

The best thing you can do is make sure that your words are deliberate and come from a place of utter confidence. This means to say things that you know to be thoughtful, careful, and meaningful.

I once had a Vice President Say things that seemed to be casual, but a few days later saw the results of such casual comments and learned that he meant what he said and had impeccable follow through. This built a tremendous amount of trust between him and me. I learned that if I trust him this much, doing this with customers may rear the same result. This goes back to casually signing up for things and then doing them with ease. It is a muscle that needs to be worked and conditioned.

Being honest and upfront is valuable for all relationships. Salespeople do a lot of talking. That is why it is incredibly important to remember what you are saying. An easy trick is to constantly say exactly what you mean and sign up for things – actions you can perform with little effort.

Speaking honestly and from a genuine place will greatly improve the conversation and ultimately build trust much faster.

When you are asked a question about your organization's ability, genuinely say what comes to mind. Do not insult your business, nor talk it down based on your personal experience, but if your company can provide the product or service, say so. Do not be blunt, rude, or insensitive. Likewise, do not give lip service for the sake of pacifying and saying yes. Be truthful and professional; this builds trust.

Also, if you do not say what you truly mean, you will experience less overall satisfaction with your situation. If your customer asks if you would like a water, and you say you do not care, you will just be thirsty in the meeting.

If you were to say, "I'd love some, actually!" Then guess what? You will get your water. It is a small example but illustrates that you are speaking honestly in all aspects.

Sometimes speaking up is uncomfortable and like other things, it is necessary and needs to be built as a habit. When you are in the habit of saying what you mean in a caring and deliberate fashion, you will go so much farther with building trust.

If we do not speak up when we are asked questions because the answer has potential to cause awkward tension that tension will just arise later in the relationship.

We sometimes dance around information or refuse to be straightforward because we do not believe our feelings to be relevant to those around us and do not want to make situations uncomfortable.

Whatever the reason, we are often very cautious communicators, but remember, honesty truly is the best policy.

Summary

- Accelerate trust.
- Be a professional.
- Elevate the experience.
- Reverse bad situations.
- Be aware of the bad stuff.
- Get to the core.
- Say what you mean.

CHAPTER 4

FEAR

"Love is the oxygen of the soul."
–Tony Robbins

Two Major Fears

The two major fears we cannot avoid are fear of not being enough and the fear of not being loved.

Whether you have been in sales for 20 years or 20 minutes, fear is a part of every sales professional's career. Having a fear of sales may seem like a sure-fire way to fail in sales, but many of the super successful in sales had the same fears that rookie sales reps and struggling professionals have. The only difference is that the super successful sales professionals have developed strategies to get beyond their fears.

Why Are We Afraid?

Love is the competitive advantage for humans. We care for our offspring in a biological way. Love is built into our basic needs.

Every species on this planet is born with a defense mechanism that protects against predators. There are some bizarre ones out there such as horns, spikes, stingers, claws, and toxins. A certain species of ant, the Malaysian exploding ant, has glands full of toxic poisons and will explode if it senses imminent danger.[4] That's wild, but we humans are born with love as a mechanism to protect each other. Oxytocin is released into the bloodstream as a hormone in response to birth. There is science behind this that helps explain why a mother spends time protecting her child until he or she is an adult (and sometimes beyond). With this biological fact, we can see how the two primal fears may come into play if we do not feel like we are good enough – or even worse, if we feel unloved. Salespeople have those fears and more specific ones as well.

Common Fears in Salespeople

The *Harvard Business Review* lists three common fears in salespeople.[6]

- Fear of not obtaining financial security
- Lack of personal ability
- Threats to social esteem

Maybe average salespeople do not take into consideration that the worst enemy is in their own thoughts. These thoughts are rooted in fear. Fortunately, there are some techniques for tackling these thoughts head on. There are techniques to get through these and I have spent a lot of time researching this and talking with lots of top sellers in all fields of sales.

If there are things successful salespeople do well, it is concealing the near debilitating terror often felt when doing the job.

Drilling down to the key attributes that separate successful salespeople from the average salesperson, the difference is fear and how they used fear in their favor instead of letting it work against them.

Fear can be defined as, "The expectation or the anticipation of possible harm."[7] But what is the harm in doing sales? Salespeople are often the antagonists in their own lives, playing against their success with negative self-talk and self-doubt. Am I good enough, smart enough? Will I win? Do they like me, or better, love me?

Other than poor sales performance, people often bail out of the profession because of fear and not because they cannot handle rejection. It is fear holding them back from picking up the phone, pushing past their comfort level, making the cold calls, walking into the lobby without an appointment, and so on. They simply do not do any of the things because they are afraid, thus not getting the results.

You Are Not Alone

Fear stalks the salesperson. There are tons of sources of fear and success is not created equally. When salespeople worry about the job, they are not worried about botching the sale. Fear of that kind doesn't go that far into the core of their being. The source can be simpler and broader, such as a fear of committing to tasks.

Instead of being on the phone trying to get a customer, you are sitting there discussing why you need to call more customers. One of the reasons why sales is so stressful is because of the quota. Missing quota means no money in your pocket, and even the potential of losing your job. The way to tackle this fear is simply activity, as we will dive deeper into later. If you know that you have done everything you could to hit your goals, then everything else is outside of your control. Activity is something you can control.

Believing that you are the only one in a sales position or on your sales team that is dealing with a fear of sales is the same as believing that you are the only one who requires oxygen. Everyone in sales has varying degrees of fear associated with their job. As stated, fears revolve around not being good enough and that ultimately leads to feeling unloved. Some fears may surround how their customers may treat them. Others may be trying to overcome their fear of delivering presentations in front of people.

After talking to hundreds of salespeople at the top of their games, and being one myself for over two decades, I have discovered a few things about the usefulness of fear. Fear acts as a primer to getting great results. One would think that a great salesperson is led by courage and confidence. Although those are common traits, one of the secret weapons I came across is using fear to get prepared. In tapping into that fear, I plan next steps, figure out how to address the bad sales calls, and remind myself to breathe. The conflict is a phenomenon that every great salesperson I spoke to insists contributes to their overall success.

As discussed earlier, not closing a sale might feel like rejection. The truth is that losing a sale means that although the customer chose a different solution, it does not necessarily mean that they did not choose you. Remember they are still buying, but they just aren't buying from you.

Furthermore, not getting a response, a meeting, or the sale seldom means you were rejected: it only means that you weren't chosen. The difference is tremendous.

When asked, "Has fear played a role in your overwhelming success?"

The answers were demonstrably and emphatically—YES.

Five Ways to Overcome Fear

Here are five ways great salespeople use the fear in the profession to outperform the competition and themselves.

1. Treat fear like a signal.

A CEO of a media company and an individual with a storied career puts it this way:

> Ultimately, fear is healthy, and it has helped drive my success in two ways.
>
> First, fear serves as a reminder that it is a signal that I need to step up to the plate and take on a new task that seems intimidating at first. Stephen Pressfield espouses that view in his book, *The War of Art*, and I wholeheartedly agree with it.
>
> Second, experiencing feelings of fear helps me to check in with the people that have looked to me for leadership (both formally and informally). I check in with them to set a vibe where they know it is perfectly fine to be fearful about Project X or Situation Y because I feel the same way from time to time. When people feel like they aren't the only one experiencing something, then above-average teamwork and productivity occurs.

Fear is telling you that the task at hand is bigger than your experience or comfort level. Successful salespeople recognize this and take on the task. Maybe it is a big account that you do not feel you can break into, or you are heading into a meeting that you are not confident in your ability to present. Use fear as an agent of change to your comfort. Tackle it head on and grow. "Fake it until you make it" is an old, outdated thought process, so be careful with it.

2. Get anxious to get prepared.

A standout saleswoman that has been a top performer for nearly a decade in her field, breaking annual records, doubling and sometimes tripling her nearest peer, uses anxiety for a preparedness check. She states, "I do anxiety really well. By envisioning worst possible outcomes, I can do things to prepare regardless if whatever could happen never actually does."

Anxiety is defined as a feeling of worry, nervousness, or unease, typically about an imminent event or something with an uncertain outcome. So, to prevent the uncertain outcome, after invoking the anxiety of what could possibly go wrong, she prepares for what is possible to go right and wins time after time.

Using the fear and anxiety as a tool is a common practice that successful salespeople use in lots of situations. Think of your presentation. Use the devil's advocate approach: poke holes in your own words, product, and presentation. Run it by your boss, mentor, co-worker, or even another customer. But try and think of ways that your message or meeting can get derailed, then practice and prepare how to get it back on track. Use this as a tool and you will eliminate the fear of something going horribly wrong. The worst case is something happens that you didn't prepare for, but now you can use that next time as a preparation tool.

3. You can fix wrong decisions but not indecision.

The fear of making the wrong move is a healthy one but not making a move at all is devastating. A real estate investor, author, and sales guru puts it this way, "There are many things that require lots of thought before action, but ultimately you have to decide and dial up a sales call and start sending prospect emails. "

Psychologist Barry Schwartz coined the phrase "paradox of choice" to describe his consistent findings that, while increased choice allows us to achieve objectively better results, it also leads to greater anxiety, indecision, paralysis, and dissatisfaction. Practice makes perfect, so call, call, call and get better along the way. The fear is what is causing the indecision.

You have to begin flexing the "just do it" muscle, then tweak the results. Being afraid to start the process will lead you nowhere.

Making decisions, learning from the mistakes, and moving forward are the differences between commotion and forward motion. So, get ready, aim, and fire!

The word "decide" comes from Latin, meaning to "cut off." When making a firm decision, you are cutting off the possibility of failing. You must know this when getting after it on the phone. You are cutting off the possibility of failure. You are cutting off the possibility of this not working.

Some people are simply intimidated by picking up the phone and calling prospects. This comes from not wanting to bother people. It is a deal breaker when it comes to sales. To get over this fear, you need to simply prepare yourself for the call and then force yourself to do it enough times where the fear wears off. After making enough calls, and understanding that even if a call goes poorly that it will not kill you, it will not be intimidating anymore, and will become second nature.

4. Kill the monster while it is small.

Taming the fear is not as much of an art form as it is a mental exercise. Identifying that fear is present, labeling it for what it is, and then determining if it is useful or not are how clinical psychologists say the skilled deal with it. The physiological presence of fear sends a signal to the adrenal glands in your torso causing them to send out cortisol and adrenaline. The fear response also releases glucose into the bloodstream—a power-up to get you running for your life. And truthfully, there are no bears chasing you in the boardroom. It all comes down to the definition laid out earlier: fear is the expectation or the anticipation of possible harm.

Psychologists will tell you that the first step in overcoming a challenge is to accept that the challenge exists. Denying that you have a fear about some part of your sales job is a great way to make sure that you either never overcome the fear or create a long delay in your mastery of your fear.

Being honest with your clients is a key element of long-term success in sales and being honest with yourself is a key element of long-term self-fulfillment.

Admitting that you have fears does require putting your ego on the back burner. Being honest about the fact that you have fears may itself reveal to you how to overcome your fear.

There is a funny thing about fears: they usually appear much larger than they are. That is precisely why this segment suggests "killing the monster" of fear while it is small. If you are an average sales rep, you tend to exaggerate fears to the point that you feel you can never overcome them.

If you take the time to pick your fears apart, you will most likely begin to see that your fear, which at one time seemed too intense to overcome, is much smaller than you thought.

Many times, your "base fear" has a host of "associated fears" that exist in your mind only because of the base fear. These associated fears were created over time and usually serve to justify your base fear to yourself. If you start to take an honest look at these associated fears, you probably will begin to feel that these aren't areas of fear for you.

Strip away enough of these associated fears, and the base fear will not seem as intimidating anymore. Biofeedback tells us that in the brain there is no biological difference between excitement and nervousness.

The human body has certain physical effects that happen inside when anxiety hits. The same exact thing happens to the body when it is anxious and afraid, and when excited. The physiological effects are indistinguishable; it is the label that gets put on it that will determine the outcome in a given situation. Neuroscientist Ian Roberts observes:

What happens when you are nervous—rapid heartbeat, sweaty skin, dry mouth, clammy palms, etc.— if you say, "I am nervous or scared," then you will perform significantly worse than if you say, "I am excited!" Just saying the words, "I am excited" versus "I am anxious" gives an 80% chance of success over failure.

So, when you begin to feel the sensations, greet the fear and welcome its effects on your body. Use it to your advantage and do not let it consume you and prevent your next move. Just know that you are in the right place and nothing bad is happening. Change the label from anxious or afraid to excited and know you are about to crush deals!

5. Breathe through it.

The most precious thing you have is your breath. The health coaches at *Think Great Lose Weight* teach a very valuable lesson: The average human can live up to three weeks without food, three days without water, but cannot survive three minutes without breath. Remember to breathe. There are two places you can check in and figure out where you are "breathing into." There are two main types of breathing: costal (meaning "of the ribs") or chest breathing, and diaphragmatic or abdominal breathing. Only when we take a maximum breath is a third variety used, known as clavicular breathing. This type of breathing is characterized by an outward, upward movement of the chest wall, your chest, or your stomach. Breathing in your chest reflects the "fight or flight," or the fear breath. Chest breathing also requires more work to be done in lifting the rib cage, thus the body must work harder to accomplish the same blood-gas mixing than with diaphragmatic breathing. The greater the work, the greater the amount of oxygen needed, which results in more frequent breaths. Chest breathing is useful during vigorous exercise, but it is quite inappropriate for ordinary, everyday activity such as sales.

Breathing into your stomach or abdomen takes a confident, assured breath and comes from a place of comfort. The principal muscle involved in abdominal breathing is the diaphragm, a strong dome-shaped sheet of muscle that separates the chest cavity from the abdomen. When we breathe in, the diaphragm contracts and pushes downwards, causing the abdominal muscles to relax and rise. In this position, the lungs expand, creating a partial vacuum, which allow air to be drawn in. When we breathe out, the diaphragm relaxes and the abdominal muscles contract to expel air containing carbon dioxide. Of the two major types of breathing, diaphragmatic breathing is the most efficient because greater expansion and ventilation occurs in the lower part of the lung where the blood perfusion is greatest. As the diaphragm contracts, it pushes the abdominal organs downwards and forwards, and this rhythmical massage gently compresses the organs and improves circulation.

If you need instruction, watch a newborn breathe. It is all in the abdomen. That baby is not afraid of making that sales call; he's in a state of calm. This type of breathing, in conjunction with physical and mental relaxation, has been found to reduce high blood pressure and anxiety significantly.

When we are calm and composed, our breathing is into the stomach or abdomen, and since there is a reciprocal relationship between breathing and the mind, practicing diaphragmatic breathing leads to mental relaxation. It is the most important tool available for stress, anxiety, or fear management. It promotes a natural, even movement of breath which both strengthens the nervous system and relaxes the body. It is the most efficient method of breathing, using minimum effort for maximum oxygen.

Check in with your breathing before and during a sales call or meeting.

Meditation teaches to focus on breath as a form of moving your focus away from the chaos of the outside world. This is true in a tough sales situation. Things may not be going your way, but just remember to breathe before speaking, breathe before reacting to the thoughts, breathe before saying something desperate. Just breathe and focus on the task at hand.

Usefulness of Fear

Fear is useful. When you are in danger, fear creates a heightened awareness of the senses. When you realize the emotion is present, harness its ability to sense if something is wrong, out of place, or needs to be said or not. Use the awareness to determine how to respond to the situation. Do not be afraid of the fear but acknowledge its presence to help guide the next compelling event. It is a useful tool and the successful people will use it that way. There are hundreds of sales methodologies and even more tactics to get the sale, but understanding your body and mind and what contributes to your success is a certain path to bigger and better success.

Summary

- People inherently have the two natural fears and they cannot avoid them: not being enough and not being loved.
- The sales process almost always puts at least one fear in conflict with the two natural fears.
- Many have come before us and have overcome these fears and the instructions are laid out in a specific order:
  - Use fear as a signal.
  - It is okay to be anxious, and you can even "get anxious to get prepared."
  - You can fix wrong decisions but not indecisions.
  - Kill the monster while it's small.
  - Breathe through it.

CHAPTER 5

Prospect

> "In the middle of every difficulty lies opportunity."
> —Albert Einstein

As many as it takes. That's the answer to the following questions:

- How many calls do I make today?
- How many emails should I send?
- How many info drops should I do?
- How many prospects should I look for?

The very first thing is you must show up. Early is the new on time. You must show up to the day every single day ready to sell. You must have the right mindset. We've talked about building trust with customers and being honest with ourselves. Activity, activity, activity is the key to going from average to the top of your game and the top of your sales force. The right activity applied to the right clients creates the right results consistently, and you must measure this. You must monitor it. You must inspect it. You must tweak it. You must make sure that you are asking for feedback and then adjusting and applying.

The right activities completed every day, and lots of them, are what create a successful salesperson. Prospecting into customers is an art form and a numbers-based game, but when done correctly, it will shorten the ramp time and truly up your game and help you reach your goals.

The Right Prospect

Identifying the right prospects is the first step. If you have something that is typically sold to a specific category of customers, it is imperative to get the right customers to prospect into. The shotgun approach may work some of the time, but it is not an effective strategy and will lengthen the time it takes to get to the right person. With all the tools available to you now, finding the right people to target and prospect to has become increasingly easier.

Search the vendor database, look for others that may sell additional services or products, and utilize your network. Use your friends, previous jobs, coaches, school affiliations, LinkedIn, Facebook, Instagram, and any other social media tools that are available and public.

Find the right prospect, verify through your tools and network that it is the right contact, and let the games begin. This is a game against yourself and the mind, against your competition, against the gatekeepers, and many other opponents. While luck may be a component of any game, you will never be lucky if you are not willing to play.

Labeling

Assigning a label to a person may limit the way you view him or her. You may inadvertently make a judgment about someone in the first few minutes of meeting him that isn't necessarily reflective of who this person is. As it pertains to your prospects and customers, this could be a costly mistake. Labeling a customer or prospect, or worse, casting a prejudiced belief, could disqualify a viable account. For example, you may believe "That used to be John's account and they do not buy," or, "This customer never buys!" There may be some truth to that, but most likely the customer is buying; they just aren't buying from you.

Labels underlie a know-it-all mentality and that kills the prospecting process. Believing that an account "will never go for this because they are not the type of account that buys" is more than likely a label that you have assigned incorrectly.

When you move into the prospecting arena, you will be able to learn for yourself what the right account is by going through a series of discovery questions, but do not label prospects prematurely because you want to skip a call. Labeling disqualifies potential customers because you are not doing the prospecting.

Measure Activity

Measured activity is crucial. Focused prospecting time during the week is also important. Some people get caught up in completing the activity, but it might not be the right kind of activity. What does that mean? Making a ton of phone calls to the wrong people is activity, but it's not going to generate any results. You haven't identified a clear-cut prospect list. You haven't identified whether these people might need your product or are even looking for a good provider of your product or service, and you are ignoring it. Or maybe you are in the other category. Maybe you are a dime a dozen. Maybe there are a lot of people who know how to sell or who may be selling what you are selling. That's going to take a little bit more of a unique approach in terms of prospecting. However, you are still going to need to do a ton of it.

You must look at your specific method of prospecting and categorize the results. When logging your activity and its result, you might think of it like a stop light: red means you haven't spoken to them and they haven't bought from you. Yellow might indicate that you have at least engaged with them but without a purchase. Green is reflective of a customer you have a relationship with who is actively buying, and this is your ultimate goal. The ability to determine which activity and how much of it resulted in a green light will enable you to replicate the process across multiple prospects to potentially generate similar results.

Categorize like this:

- Those I believe would buy, but to whom I have not yet sent any communication.
- Those to whom I've sent some method of communication, but have not yet responded to me.
- Those who have responded to me, but I have not yet met with or discussed my product or offering.
- Those who are in communication with me, but have not purchased.
- Those who have purchased once, but not a second time.

Try organizing your sales process using some version of these categories. Doing so will translate your sales approach from a red light to a green light.

When you start your day, start with those prospects you are already communicating with and then move down the list. You want to build a big customer base through prospecting.

Communication

Call, email, send LinkedIn messages, set up events, attend networking events, and use your affiliations. Do anything you can to get close to your prospect and give them your clear, crisp pitch. Do as much of it as possible without being annoying. Rotate out your prospecting list so that you aren't doing too much of it to the same company or person.

What to say on a cold call? Let's look at an example:

"Hey Mr. Customer,

Sorry to barge in on your day but this should only take a few seconds. Look, I despise cold calling and I bet you do not like answering them either—so I want to only spend a few minutes to see if our organizations are able to do business together."

More than likely they will appreciate the honesty and begin the discussion. I used to get, "Well, what do you do?" and that kicked off the conversation.

What to write on an email? The average executive gets over 300 emails a day. Use brevity and get straight to the point. Do not start by saying, "Hope all is well!"

"Mr. Customer,

I've called and left you a few messages and figured email may get a quicker response. I have identified that many in your industry are working with my organization to solve problems that you may be experiencing as well. Please call me or let me know when might be a good time to connect, as time is of the essence.

I look forward to your response."

What to write on a LinkedIn message?

"Looks like you and I share some common connections. Here is my product or service. I would like an opportunity to talk with you as I believe you may find it to be a great fit. Many in your industry use my organization to solve problems that you may also be

experiencing. Please let me know when you have a moment to connect.

Best, [Your Name]"

Identifying through your own research and due diligence how your product or service may help will show that you are prepared and disciplined in your approach.

The Tale of Two Stories

Story #1 – You finally land a 30-minute meeting with the right prospect. You show up on time and you walk into the conference room. They have decided to bring a few colleagues that may have an interest in doing business with you.

You ask if there is a projector and that is the only question you ask. You plug in your device and open a Microsoft PowerPoint presentation. You spend 20 minutes sharing all of your content to let them know how awesome your company is and how much they need you.

The customer looks at his phone mid-way through and you lose the room. You wrap up, reminding them there are lots of areas you can help, thank them, and leave.

You never hear from them again. You have wasted an opportunity and lost the ability to truly deliver value.

Today's customer is extremely knowledgeable, and markets are increasingly competitive. The successful sales rep knows that Story #1 is an old and outdated way of going about things and there is zero chance that you will get anywhere using that pitiful technique.

Story #2 – You finally land a 30-minute meeting with the right prospect. You have done your research and, based on your adapting technique, have shown up appropriately, dressed in a suit and tie, based on their dress code.

You show up on time and walk into the conference room. They have decided to bring a few colleagues that may have an interest in doing business with you.

You begin the meeting by reviewing their core values and mission statement and relate it back to your own. You continue the meeting letting them know that you have spent some time with some of their subordinates and associated vendors and have identified a few areas that you can help. You ask a few open-ended questions to validate whether these areas are correct, and if so, continue by aligning your product or service to their needs and initiatives. At the tail end, you mention you have slides, if they are still interested. You then spend a few minutes hitting the high-level points but by now they are convinced that you can hop right in and assist.

I wonder which one would work?

Measure Customers

The second portion of activity is to track your actual sales. Measure your sales contacts and begin to increase both simultaneously. Remember this book is not meant to teach you how to sell. It's meant to provide examples from real people who are top sellers. Successful salespeople mechanically override the shotgun approach. They do not just pick up the phone and start making dials, then forget who they call. I'm fairly certain that you have some form of CRM system that you can track and measure your activity and results as we talked about in the previous section.

Now what we want to look at is your actual sales data. You want to convert those prospects into buying customers and keep the ones you already have.

Building a loyal customer base is one of the highest forms of creating a super successful sales book of business. Regardless of what you are selling, the most important thing that you can remember is to do great work consistently, so your customers will continue to buy from you and hopefully refer you to other potential customers.

It cannot be said enough. Success begins with activity, activity, activity. Keep selling to your existing customers and repeat. Make sure you understand why they are buying from you and replicate the process.

The right activity and the right customers drive the right results. You must be able to create the right activity. That means prospecting into the right accounts consistently and what to say when you are prospecting. Which demographic has a high consumption of your product? Where are your customers? How are they buying? You do not have to invest any money in this. You can find this on social media. You can find a wealth of information on LinkedIn. Look online for articles and updates on the trade. Become an expert.

Practice

Make sure you are practicing your pitch consistently every single day. You should be studying and refining your script, whether that means you are recording your calls and critiquing yourself, practicing in the mirror or on your friends or family for feedback. It may feel obnoxious, but you are practicing being at the top of your game and this requires repetition and refinement. This book is for those who want to be the best of the best. This is what the best of the best do. Practice makes perfect. Repetition, perfect practice, asking for feedback, and continuing to learn and grow.

I spent a lot of time with a friend who started a new organization. After about three months, she still couldn't pitch me a crisp and clean explanation of what her organization did, and she was in sales. I suggested that she really needed to be able to articulate what she was trying to accomplish if she was going to be selling it. You need to know thoroughly what you are selling in order to sell a lot of it. That means the right activity starts with making sure you know exactly what it is you are selling and then practicing that pitch over and over. That sounds obvious, but there are plenty who start jobs in sales and think that their sales are going to be good because of some prior success in a previous role; they didn't necessarily invest all the time it took to get to the next level. After finishing this book, I want you to be able analyze your past in this new light. This is not generic information. This is very specific information that has come from the top salespeople across many different platforms and verticals who have been at the top of their game. This is what they do over and over again, even as they move into new roles at new companies.

The right activity starts with knowing what you are selling. To know your product or service well, you must practice pitching what you are selling. You do not have to be a technical expert, but you absolutely need to be able to articulate very crisply and cleanly in 30 seconds or less, or about five sentences. Get after it.

Start spreading the message. You must prospect correctly. You must prospect into the right accounts. You must identify who the right people are or who the right departments are that purchase your product or service. Practice your pitch, research who it is that buys your stuff, and who needs your services. If you are prospecting into the wrong department or to the wrong person and they're not responding to you, you are going to mistake activity with progress. You are going to think "I made my 50 to 100 calls today." But if 90% of those calls were made to the wrong people, then you are going backwards because you are wasting valuable time prospecting into the wrong accounts or reaching out to the wrong people.

Increase Your Customer Base

If you have the resources, you may find value in some form of a sales database or prospect list. A few to consider are *DiscoverOrg* or

Gartner. These are generally not very expensive. Keep your CRM tight! Log every phone number and correct email address into your phone and CRM with notes for every single contact and repeat. Make sure you are logging them every time. Those who I've known that have been at the top of their game know how important CRM hygiene is, and how to pivot into different segments of the business to get different contacts and diversify the way that they sell into their customers.

Every time that you get a new or prospect, make sure you are logging that into your CRM or phone. Make sure that you are recording it and putting some form of note in it, taking the next step to begin prospecting into each one.

Ask your current buying customers for introductions and referrals into other accounts. Do not be shy; you are a salesperson asking for more ways to do your job. Take pride in doing this and do it with confidence.

Find Ways to Connect

One of the key things that define the right activity is to make sure that when talking to your customers, it's not always an attempt to sell them something. This goes back to building a good relationship. I was told by a large restaurant chain in my territory that, "If each time that you call me it's about sales, we're not building the right type of relationship." Incorporate social conversation into your prospecting activity. Perhaps remember to mail a card on their birthday. Let them know they are in front of your mind by sending them articles that are relevant to their interests, both personal and professional. Do not forget what you have read about in terms of building trust and rapport, such as discussing sports teams, hobbies, and periodicals or news about their organization.

One way I was able to grow a professional relationship was sending a press conference to my customer and then asking them, "Did you know about this before it hit the press? Just curious on how internal communications works." The customer responded back to me and said, "Thanks for sending this to me. I had no idea that this was going on. Proof that our internal communication is not very prevalent here." I followed that back up with, "I understand. There are a lot of things that I do not know about as well. Typical. Hey, let's grab some lunch," and then I pivoted into something different. There's a big component to the activity that does not have to do with sales.

Networking with social hours, happy hours, dinners, and lunches are all events that play into this. Make sure you are reserving time to spend quality time with your customer that has nothing to do with the sale. You must be able to separate who you are as a person from who you are as a business associate. Show them who you are through activity. Send them notes about whatever you feel is relevant to them. Call them and talk to them. Keep it brief.

Summary

- Early is the new on time. You must show up to the day every single day ready to sell. Be ready to prospect and plan for it. Do not make this a casual occurrence that you may get to. Plan for it and do it.
- Identify the right prospects by searching through all the various tools, online social media outlets, vendors, friends, and family.
- Prospect all day in all ways – calls, emails, LinkedIn, etc. Send the right message, keep it short and to the point. Make sure you are doing your research and be relevant.
- Land the meeting, use the adapting technique, and be prepared. Use your research to connect with the customer on their level and tie back their mission and core values to your positioning.

CHAPTER 6

Keep Going

"Many of life's failures are people who did not realize how close they were to success when they gave up."
—Thomas A. Edison

- Do a mental check in right now – where are you?
- Is your breathing coming from the chest or belly?
- How is your confidence and self-talk?
- Where is your activity?
- Are you pushing forward or are you stuck?
- Are you close and just do not know it?

Do not disguise yourself as a salesperson. You are a salesperson. Your customers know this and if you do it correctly, they will value you beyond belief. Never forget that your role is to earn the right, privilege, honor, and respect to meet with each customer and gain their trust in you and your solution to their problem.

You must have the passion to serve and the desire to improve your customer's life through your product or service.

During this chapter you are going to learn how to "keep moving forward." You begin with passion, then you will begin to see progress, while maintaining your enthusiasm. You have moved through some old limitations and now you are on fire. But momentum fades, and you still run the risk of settling back into the habit of fear and mediocrity.

This happens to the best of us, so know that you are not alone. Lots of folks, even the top performers, inevitably fall into a rut. We will begin with exercises to help get out of the rut and keep moving forward. Because the worst disappointment is to be so close to a goal and then giving up.

This will not happen to you because this chapter will teach you how to keep moving forward. Perseverance will prevail.

Where Are You?

Has your self-talk devolved to being negative and anti-progressive? Have you struck out a few times and forgot the numbers game? Have you forgot to gamify the process? Have you stopped having fun? Well get up and dance, make a funny noise, or do anything that reminds you that you are in the business of communicating with other human beings and you must be a positive force.

One of Don Miguel Ruiz's *Four Agreements* is: "Always do your best."[8] Do the best you can and have no regrets. Have patience with yourself. Be consistent and persistent and make sure your actions are meaningful. Some days, your best won't be good as it is other days, and that's okay. Put an honest effort into life and you will not end up feeling ashamed. Do not beat yourself up over a less-than-stellar performance. Simply always strive to do your best.

Are you pushing forward or are you stuck? Are you making headway despite some difficulty, self-doubt, and negative outcomes?

Ultimately, the goal is to keep moving forward towards your goal regardless of roadblocks, obstacles, made-up excuses, flat tires, personal problems, financial woes, etc. The goal is to keep going.

Some days will be better than others. Keep this in mind and try not to beat yourself up if something isn't going your way. This, too, shall pass. If you are having a bad day, remember that it will not be that way for long, and the same goes for good days.

Is your breathing coming from the chest or belly? If you need to know the secret, visit my good friends over at *Think Great Lose Weight*. Brian Johnson can help assess whether your breathing is in harmony or not. Remember to breathe. If it is coming as a shallow chest breath, stand up, take a deep belly breath and exhale with vigor. Now make a call.

Where is your activity? Review your activity and your methods of tracking. Did you start your day, week, and month with a firm understanding that measuring activity is a sure-fire way of managing it? Can you actually see the customers moving from one category to the next? Re-evaluate your prospect list and make sure that the ones you are calling are the ones who can buy. Remember there is a huge difference between forward motion and commotion. If you are kicking up a bunch of dust but not progressing towards your goal of selling your solution, then stop and re-evaluate your approach. Make the appropriate adjustments and keep moving forward.

Do not give up. The worst pain one can experience is being so close and then giving up. It will cause a lifetime of regret. Regret is like being handed a suitcase of bricks you have to carry: heavy, but useless. Getting past this phase takes a strong will to survive. Do not surrender to excuses, do not retreat to mediocrity, and do not stop the progress. Do not stop in the path, and for God's sake, do not turn around! Are you close and just do not know it? This takes extreme honesty, fortitude, and courage in pain or adversity.

Our greatest weakness lies in giving up and the most certain way to succeed is always to try just one more time."
—Thomas A. Edison

Burn the Boats

In 1519, Spanish conquistador Hernán Cortés landed in what is now Mexico. He then ordered his men to burn the boats.[9] This forced the men to face the fact that the only alternative to winning was death. If the boats remained docked nearby, the men maintained the option to retreat. Are you holding onto excuses that are allowing you to continue to fail to move forward? Are you putting obstacles in the way of your own success? These are your boats. You must burn them to ashes and never let them get in your way again. You cannot board excuses and use them to retreat from certain victory. Ask yourself, "How am I going to win? What must I do right now to begin moving forward? Am I willing to burn my boat so there is no alternative to success?" This is a quest! This is not easy. What might you be doing that is causing commotion but not forward motion? What must you stop doing RIGHT NOW in order to move forward?

Set the Right Goals

Start with easy goals that you know you can achieve. Remember you can get things done when you set your mind to it.

Here is a quick example: Put a stick, pole, broom, or any object that can serve as a line on the ground. Walk a step back, close your eyes, and visualize yourself leaping over the stick. Now open your eyes, take a giant one-legged leap forward, and get over your goal. How easy was that? You just set a goal and conquered it. You are probably thinking, "That was too easy!" Now set an easy work goal and follow it through until completion.

Make the goal an easy one and get past it. "I want to get in contact with the lead buyer today." Or, "I want to retrieve this piece of information that will help me finalize this deal."

Stack them up, write them down, and get after them. Be grateful that you are moving through your goal list and keep moving forward. Start with something as simple as spending the first 15 minutes calling your existing customers and thanking them for their business. The goal is to create achievement. Success breeds success, and it is awesome to witness how achieving one goal will prompt you to feel more challenged to move to the next one.

Look for Progress, Not Perfection

Do not let tasks linger. This includes calls to be returned, emails to be read, and anything else you need to get off your plate. We all suffer at one time or another from feeling overwhelmed with everything, and when we do, our level of motivation will simply diminish.

When you first wake up, write down three things you are thankful for in the job you get to do each day. This is a method of priming for a good day as well as a reminder to focus and get the right mindset. Look for progress, not perfection. People pursue progress in a lot of areas, whether it is fitness, in a relationship, etc.

You could certainly do it while at work as well. Progress in sales is easy to pick up on. Are your customers responding to you? Do they leave clues that they want to buy? Are they asking you certain questions about your product or your services that may lead to a buying decision? Are you getting more responses than non-responses? Are you getting more face-to-face meetings? Are your sales starting to stack up? These are all indicators of progress.

You might do the same thing in a relationship. You call somebody. They call you back. You begin texting. You start to increase the communication, and thus the trust. Then you begin to increase the amount of time you are seeing each other. That's progress. The same goes in fitness and weight loss. Am I gaining muscle? Am I losing weight? That's progress.

Things are not going happen overnight, but incrementally. If you are able to review where you started and where you are now, then you can evaluate the progress. If you are not making progress, or if there's no clear indication that progress is present, re-evaluate your actual activity. Are you calling out to the right people? Are you sending the right types of email messages? Are you visiting with your mentor or your Roger Bannister enough?

The one thing that I learned early on is that you must plant a lot of seeds. You must let things take hold. If I plant a seed, water it, and expose it to the right amount sunlight, then I will begin to see the progress. But I must plant plenty of seeds if I want plenty of fruit. My mentor told me long ago that after planting the seed, I cannot go back and dig up the seed to see if it is growing. That's disturbing the process. You will be able to evaluate the progress as you start to see that tree grow, and ultimately it will bear fruit.

Forensic Feedback

Now, as we begin to evaluate progress, we need to make sure that we are forensically investigating and inspecting feedback.

If your customers are providing direct feedback, it is easy to diagnose and rectify. But if you keep doing what you are doing, and it is not working, you truly need to investigate your approach and make the necessary changes for it to begin working. The forensic portion of the feedback is to evaluate everything. Take a step back and look at the whole picture. Really ask yourself if you would want to buy from yourself right now?

Forensic feedback means investigating every aspect of the feedback you receive and inspecting exactly what you are doing. The goal is to be candid with yourself about what is working and what is not. If you are receiving little or no response from any of the emails you send, or if they've slowed down, are you sending enough? Are you including the right content? Have you been sending fewer emails than you did when you started this book? You must be able to clearly identify the problem without outside feedback and start addressing the potential problems.

If you are getting negative responses, look at the feedback. If you are getting positive responses but not much of it, make sure that you are calling your customers and asking them very specifically for feedback and why they chose to buy from you. Listen to the feedback in a forensic manner.

If you look at a forensic investigator, they take in every detail. They look at the weather. They look at hair follicles. They look at footprints. They look at everything when they are investigating a crime scene, and you must do the same thing. You must forensically investigate every single aspect of your success or lack thereof.

If your progress has slowed, review yourself, review your attitude. Are you in a good mood? Are you in a bad mood? Are you stressed out? Not hitting your quota is a stressful experience. Is something in your way, and if so, why did that stop you? Ask yourself very clearly whether you are allowing yourself to get your own way. Review every communication. Review the tone of it, the nature, the grammar, the punctuation, and really look at all the elements you need to make it work.

Take a step back and look at the progress. Forensically investigate everything that is going on in your book of business, your day-to-day function. Look at it and provide yourself with clear, honest feedback so you can adjust and continue to move forward.

Control the Controllable

Controlling the controllable is very closely related to forensic feedback. However, now you are identifying the actions that take place day to day. Look at the things that you can under a microscope. There are more things within your control than you may be aware. For instance, when did your day begin? Can you control that? If you have a lot to do in the morning that does not contribute to your success in sales, wake up earlier. You can control that. Do not put excuses in the way and call them the uncontrollable. You can control how many phone calls you make, emails you send, prospecting visits you make, and vendor communications you engage in. You can control your numbers. You can control your activity. Some things that are uncontrollable, such as a sick customer or your customer's bad mood, are all possibilities on any given day. But by focusing on the things you can control, you will ensure your success, even when things do not go your way all the time.

The point is not to let silly excuses get in the way and tell yourself, "There's nothing I can do about this." You can control your attitude. You can control your thoughts. You can control whether you are being distracted by social media, spending too much time on your phone, being lazy, or procrastinating. All of these pitfalls are controllable. If you are engaged in any of this negative behavior, do not give it false control. Do not tell yourself, "I guess I just have a lack of focus, so I cannot do this." That's wrong. You can focus on the things that are most important to you and get through it. This is controlling the controllable.

Evaluate everything you can control. It is not as obvious as you think. You must become conscious of the perceived uncontrollable to start controlling it. Evaluate the uncontrollable and identify ways to avoid it in the future.

Reward Yourself Because You Deserve It

It is 5 p.m. on the last day of the month or quarter. The lower 80% have left the office or they are at a bar nearby celebrating because they barely met quota. The successful are in the office. They've already hit their goal, but they are still sending emails, scheduling meetings, and making calls. And by laying the foundation for a great month before they need to, they always blow their goals out of the water.

Rewarding yourself is key as a top performer but rewarding yourself for mediocrity will keep you mediocre. Do not prematurely reward yourself. Do not congratulate yourself for simply doing the bare minimum required for your job. Get past that limited mentality and get to the great rewards.

Set a big goal for yourself and go after it. Tie a reward to successfully reaching that goal:

> If I close this deal, then I will do X, Y, Z.

Make it very near and dear to your heart and restrict yourself from engaging in the reward until you have accomplished the goal. It is my favorite part of the job. I reward myself with trips and fancy dinners and nice things. I reward myself with contribution and giving to others. I reward myself with bringing other people over the bridge of fire. I find it incredibly rewarding to set goals, get after it each day with intense vigor, and then cross the finish line because I know that there is something to look forward to when I succeed in reaching the goal I set for myself. There's massive reward outside of the incentives I set for myself as well, such as stature, notoriety, President's Club trips, awards, and the respect of my peers. There are other potential rewards that are motivating as well, such as additional business from existing customers and client referrals. The other rewards of being successful include intrinsic rewards such as having a healthy self-esteem. Make sure you are paying attention to all rewards that come from success because during our next chapter, we are going to talk about what it is like to be at the top.

Daily Practices Build Monthly Results

End each day celebrating the most significant accomplishment, regardless of how small or trivial it might appear to be.
Reward yourself. You can even be motivated by the instant gratification you receive from an email response, setting a meeting, and making a sale. Do not forget to celebrate each win and reward yourself.

You are almost there. You have very clear, specific ways to create success. We have defined what you should be focusing on, how your belief system should work, what the activity should look like, what to say on email, how to send LinkedIn messages, and what to say on a cold call. We have provided enough information to you to keep moving forward and toward success. We have determined what the right activity looks like, how to measure that activity, your sales behavior, and your sales numbers. We have addressed avoiding distractions and how to control the controllable. We have discussed how to forensically investigate the activity that you are doing and provide specific feedback, either from your customers or to yourself, and we have talked about getting past any type of false obstacles keeping you from ultimate success.

Successful salespeople always look at themselves as their biggest competition. They do not make excuses. They do not consider the actual competition. They are continuously introspective. They wake up each morning with the mindset that it is them against themselves. They understand if they are engaged in the right behavior from beginning to end, they are going to beat their competition, as well as beat their previous performance, and that is the goal. On the following page, write down some goals right now while the thought is in your head. Say them out loud, and who cares if anyone is around to hear you. Do it!

Summary

- Check in.
- Set the right goals.
- Burn the boats.
- Look for progress, not perfection.
- Perform forensic feedback.
- Control the controllable.
- Reward yourself.
- Build a daily practice.

CHAPTER 7

LET GO OF THE EGO

"The ego is only an illusion, but a very influential one. Letting the ego-illusion become your identity can prevent you from knowing your true self."
—Wayne Dyer

This is a very important chapter. In fact, it may be the most important chapter in this book.

You have done it all right. You have identified the right contacts, reached out in thoughtful ways, adapted to the customer's needs, did the research, got the meeting, nailed the content, and addressed their problem: you have arrived. You are winning, and winning consistently.

Success does different things to different people, but one of the precursors to success is work (and lots of it). Success does not come easy. It is not attained by all people due to their lack of resilience, perseverance, and grit.

Success should never be a surprise. It is a logical next step for sticking to something and accomplishing your goal. It is a logical next phase to all that you have done since beginning this book. But once you cross the line of success, you must understand that what got you here is what is going to keep you here. Albeit, you have already carved a path, and now you are on the road to success, but you must continue taking that road and forging new paths to bigger and better success.

The success tax in the sales world is heavy. Lots of people do not want to pay it. For many, once they begin to enjoy some level of success, they may begin to think that since they've already reached their goal, there is no reason to continue the behaviors they employed to reach the goal. The success tax requires you to avoid that mentality and continue the process to remain successful.
The ego is the part of the brain that is entitled, arrogant, and off-putting to most people. The ego is a component of success that most wish they could alleviate, but the reality is the ego is alive and well.

Sometimes, the ego outgrows the rational mind and kills success. I strategically placed "Let Go of the Ego" toward the end of this book because ultimately, you will need to re-evaluate your success after it starts to happen consistently.

The ego is a natural enemy to successful people. Many perceive successful salespeople as having a big ego, and sometimes that may be true. But understand that it is a predator to success. It will come after you and slip in when you least expect it and cause catastrophic failure if you allow it to take over. Letting go of the ego is not easy once it has a grip on successful people. But during this chapter, we will go step by step on how to let go of it.

When I come across an egotistical, pseudo-successful salesperson, I am literally counting the days before they begin to decline because egotism is the antithesis to success. You sell stuff and happen to align the correct people who need your solution, and you do it more than anybody else. When looked at from that perspective, it quickly inflates the ego, and helps you realize that you are doing a great job, but let's not forget that others can do it too.

You are matching the right number of prospective clients with a solution to their problem. That is a good start, but that's no reason to falsely inflate your ego and make yourself out to be Superman. If you are doing it well and following the steps discussed in past chapters, you will be ramping up your sales. There's no reason to start touting your abilities as if you are better than the next person, because that is what will kill success in a heartbeat.

Another facet of the ego and how it diminishes success is by alienating your customers, who would otherwise want to help you. Once you appear arrogant to these customers, they will not tell you this, but they will likely begin avoiding your calls. They may realize their confidence in you could be contributing to your inflated ego, so they may choose to stop buying from you. This is how ego slips in and causes catastrophic damage. You are listening to your ego and do not recognize that you are offending the people around you by being an egotistical jerk.

Ego is Expensive

Now, how do you let go of it? Start by acknowledging the fact that your ego is getting in the way. Ask for feedback. Evaluate your actions and your words. Evaluate your attire. Are you starting to dress differently, act differently, talk differently? Are you not paying attention to the details? Are you moving away from some of the mundane things that you did so extraordinarily well in the beginning? Are you slowing down now because you feel like those types of activities are beneath you? That is the biggest lesson that you can take away from letting go of the ego.

At one point in time, you were in the middle of the pack, suffering and not knowing how to get to the top, so you were answering every phone call with enthusiasm, hoping that there was an opportunity there. Now when the phone rings at 4:45 p.m. on a

Friday afternoon, and perhaps you are headed to a happy hour, do you still decide to pick it up? If not, why?

Because you are not as hungry as you used to be. You start to take off in the middle of the day. You spend more time during the day shopping online. You start to post things on social media as if you are now more important. Why? Because customers have decided to buy your product or service after you have engaged in the right behaviors.

Do not oversell your abilities because you have now been able to consistently put your product and service in front of a bunch of people that need it. Remember to reward yourself. Remember to be proud of what you do, but stay humble. Do not be an egotistical jerk because nobody wants to hang around with that guy or girl.

Another way of identifying ego is not meeting with people that you used to meet with. Or maybe when you do meet with them, you show up a few minutes late. You feel entitled. You think you are the most important person in the room. You've sold the most. You are their most valuable salesperson, so you start to show disrespect by not being on time, being less attentive, or maybe not remaining hungry. You may not be paying attention to the people in the room, but the people in the room are certainly paying attention to you. This is expensive because it costs you customers.

Sometimes customers that call on a Friday afternoon have an urgent need. The person hungry for success will answer that call 10 times out of 10. The egotistical, bloated successful person now tends to decline that call, because they believe the customer is too needy. They may be thinking, "I cannot waste my time. It is Friday afternoon," forgetting that working deep into Friday was a component of the start of their success.

Lessons Learned

There are many lessons to be learned about your journey to success. You were able to overcome seemingly insurmountable obstacles, so do not waste that by thinking you are better than others. Avoid regret and pride. Do not feel sorry for anything you discover about yourself. Continue to focus on your efforts and not on the past outcomes. Stop telling yourself the false narrative that you deserve this and that is what makes you better than others. There is no grand narrative. You have put forth effort and have arrived at your destination. You have achieved your desired goal. You are at the top. It is important to stay there, so avoid succumbing to an over-weening ego.

The longest and biggest journey to success will be determined by avoiding the pitfalls of egotism. You ride the pendulum on the way up, but you will also ride the pendulum on the way down. Being able to hop off the pendulum of ego will shorten these swings. The higher you swing up in celebration, the lower you swing down in desperation if something doesn't go your way. Avoid the ego and the self-entitled mentality of, "I deserve this because I am the best," as that is the fastest way to kill your momentum.

Truthfully, if you are representing a quality product or service and you are representing yourself well, the customer will buy into that.

God Complex

A God complex is a belief characterized by consistently inflated feelings of personal ability, privilege, or infallibility.[10] A person with a God complex may refuse to admit the possibility of their error or failure, even in the face of irrefutable evidence, intractable problems, or difficult or impossible tasks.

Having a God complex is a real problem when it comes to crossing over the line of success. If you are lucky, you will remember the pain of being in the bottom or the middle of the pack and will fight to stay at the top and catch the ego early. Train yourself down and make sure you are doing the work.

Become obsessed with humility. Read books about the great heroes and mimic their humility. Be humble because everyone laughs at the ego when it falls. The great chess player, Bobby Fischer, once said, "I like the moment I break a man's ego." It's a scary thought, and no doubt led to his status as a pariah. But everyone wants to see the ego destroyed. The ego is a fleeting friend. Once it is no longer fed, it leaves faster than a fair-weather fan. If you are not stoking your ego with self-proclamation of grandeur, then it will begin to starve and eventually die, and then you can maintain and even exceed your success.

How to Eliminate the Ego

Be still. I know this is a simple statement but take a moment and focus on the right here and right now. You have come a long way and it is right and proper to be proud. We must recognize and dissolve the ego. Being present in the moment will quickly rid your thoughts of self-importance. Be extremely grateful and appreciative that you are where you are because of your great effort. But assign no significance to the moment. Whether you just checked into a five-star hotel and came from an important meeting or are about to board first class on a flight, try to avoid thinking what a badass you are, and instead, focus on how appreciative you are of the comfort success brings.

Recognizing things that label power, prestige, and status will quickly inflate the ego. Believing you are the best is not only not true, but it will ultimately hurt you. Instead reword that self-talk to, "I seek to consistently provide excellent support to my customers and will be recognized when I do it well."

The ego will blind you, so do not listen to it. Remind yourself daily that it was your hunger and passion that got you to where you are now, and maintaining that same effort will keep you here. This is very important because the ego leaves quickly if it is not being fed. You have a great product or service and a passion to exemplify its benefits to your customers consistently. Learn this and make sure you are giving gratitude in all areas.

Give More to Get More

Give more appreciation and you will receive more to appreciate. Demonstrating this day to day is one of my favorite things. Smile at people and you will get one back.

The law of circulation is the flow of energy that we put into the world. It's the belief that what we give is what we can expect to receive. If you cut the stem in half, the flower will never bloom. You have not allowed the circulation to take place. Put simply, if they say, "Thank you," and you do not say, "You are welcome," you are less likely to get another thank you. You have cut off the reciprocation and circulation. The circulatory system is what keeps things alive in the body, in life, and in sales.

If the customer gives to you, make every effort to receive and give back.

Now what does this have to do with the ego? The ego is entitled and feels deserving of the "give" from others and will not say thank you. It will not reciprocate. It will not recognize that it may be a gift that is being given and will not even have the decency to say thank you. This is a very pitiful and sad event to watch because the ego has taken over and the egotistical person will bounce, and bounce hard.

When entrenched with the being of ego, one is mesmerized – even seduced – into thinking that he or she is better and more deserving. This may last for a short while, but the natural laws of reciprocity and circulation will stop providing because it is nature's way. The law of reciprocity is basically when someone does something nice for you, you will have an urge to do something nice in return. You may even reciprocate with a gesture more generous than their original good deed.

It is important to research your own actions, true abilities, and results and compare them to your perception. The ego is a dangerous tool and usually used as a weapon against low self-esteem.

Confidence vs. Ego

There is something to be said about having confidence. I do not want to contradict the message by making it seem that confidence is a bad thing, but an inflated ego must not be mistaken for confidence. When you are in the middle of the pack and in the process of moving to the top, sometimes overconfidence spills into being egotistical.

Confidence is the trust that you can do what you set out to do. The word "confidence" literally translates to "firmly trusting and boldness."

Ego is the opposite of being confident. The ego is a second self that shows up and ruins everything. It is a big problem when it comes to getting to be a top salesperson.

Chances are that you know some of these egotistical people – not to be confused with the confident ones. The egotistical one will be extremely braggadocious and cocky. And this really does nothing for their sales career.

Having a healthy amount of confidence is necessary, but confidence is built by accomplishing goals, learning new skills, identifying solutions, and getting it done. Building the muscle of execution garners confidence. But blurring the lines between confidence and cockiness or ego is an easy mistake, and you must constantly check yourself to avoid being on the wrong side of that line.

Consider asking someone you trust to be your accountability partner. Having somebody that cares enough to tell you the truth and ground you is priceless. These people remind you of your value and recognize your talent, but conversely, aren't afraid to tell you when you are acting like a fool.

You are not better than anybody else. You are only better than who you used to be. Make sure that you stay grounded in your accomplishments because the ego will draw you backwards rather than move you forward.

To wrap up, the over-inflated ego will completely strip away your confidence if you are ever put in your place by a customer. This is incredibly awkward and uncomfortable. If a customer calls you out on your behavior, it could reverse any type of success you've enjoyed, and cause you to question everything because now your self-esteem has taken a hit.

When you get direct feedback on your egotistical personality, you start to question every word you say in every interaction that you have. Do not let it get to this point. Be certain that you are keeping a healthy self-esteem, remaining confident, and continuing to do what you say you are going to do. Above all, stay humble.

Remember, you get what you give.

There are a number of books about the ego. One of my favorites is *The Power of Now* by Eckhart Tolle. Tolle explains the ego as the pain body, or the pain that we have in trying to be somebody in the eyes of other people. We attempt to satisfy the ego by behaving a certain way. Not only is it off-putting to other people around us, but it's extremely detrimental to ourselves, because it will eventually destroy any confidence that we have built through the hard work that we have done.

Having a healthy amount of confidence is important and demonstrates the fact that you can execute for your customers. But be cautious of confusing a bloated ego with having a healthy amount of confidence.

Summary

- Ego is imaginary and expensive.
- Absorb your lessons learned.
- Avoid the God complex.
- Constantly check-in to eliminate the ego.
- Give more to get more.

CHAPTER 8

GET A JACKET

> "Knowing yourself is the beginning of all wisdom."
> —Aristotle

This last chapter is called "Get a Jacket" for a reason. It is my favorite chapter because this is celebrating the fact that you have become a successful salesperson by working very hard. You have done everything that you set out to do. You have built great habits. You are documenting your progress. You are paying attention to the details. You have a healthy self-confidence and the bold trust that you can execute for your customers on a consistent basis. And most importantly, you realize that it is not very hard to do once you do it.

This is an emotional chapter because you have realized that your own limiting thoughts and beliefs have been your biggest adversary all along. The biggest enemy that we face is ourselves. Believing in yourself can be the most difficult when you are going up against what is seemingly impossible.

This chapter will move through some reminders of what it takes to get to the top, but also what your duty is now that you are here.

Biggest Bridge of Fire

Writing this book was my biggest bridge of fire. I had to reach deep down inside and learn that my biggest adversary was myself – my own personal critic, the voice inside of my head telling me that I am not good enough – and that this is not good enough. *Nobody's going to read this book. It is garbage.* And I had to keep pressing on despite those voices and negative thoughts.

But what I realized is my biggest duty after becoming a successful salesperson is to help those around me cross their own bridges of fire. This is a very difficult job to do when you are in the thick of it. The struggle is real. But the important thing is to find the help you need to get started, and that's the reason I chose to write this book.

I want to help. I want to teach that belief is a key component to getting across the bridge of fire and that everybody is afraid of it. I wanted to illustrate that there are techniques like modeling and adapting and there are things to avoid like labeling. But the biggest lesson is to make sure that you are equipped to handle the struggle. Because you will face struggle, and the biggest struggle is against yourself.

Going up against yourself is going to be the toughest competitor you have ever faced, more so than someone selling a competing solution. Your competition could go up against you in every meeting, and you would still be the real adversary.

When I first started my career, I really didn't know much. I had several offers of help and I was skeptical. I was filled with reasons why I knew more than they did, and I had the excuses to prove it. Some people allowed me to believe it, but others pressed me to question my own beliefs. Some called me on my delusions and stated upfront and loudly that as long as I believed that, I would never go any further than where I was at that moment.

Many of those who helped me had nothing to gain for themselves. And after dozens of these people helped me, I realized that there was a trait they all shared: they, themselves, had crossed their own bridges of fire. What I have found by being in their company is that they felt it was their duty to help others who had a desire to be better. I now find that I feel the same duty.

The primary reason I am sharing this with you is because I feel an obligation to help. The tips and tricks that I have built over a quarter century of sales success were built because I had dozens of people who were willing to show me how to do it. There was nothing in it for them other than the satisfaction of helping somebody else cross the bridge of fire.

I have realized that as much as my own personal mentors wanted to see me succeed and as much as I want to see others succeed, there is one consistent truth: no one can do it for anybody else. You must do it for yourself. You must learn the techniques, you must study the material, and ultimately, you must do the hard work yourself. And it is tough. The first chapter talks about mindset. If you have never been able to accomplish what you set out to accomplish, it is hard to believe that you can accomplish it. That's why it is important find your role models. Find your own Roger Bannister.

Treasure Your Mentors

When you find people around that are willing to help you, latch on to them. Do not let them go. Be grateful that they are there. Continue to align yourself with successful people and they will help you stay on track. Listen to what they have to say. Gear up and build the fortitude to get over the bridge of fire because the other side is extremely rewarding.

Getting over it is very difficult. You may be only a few months away or a week away. But even if you are a year away, you are only 365 days away from changing your life. Understand that once you cross the bridge of fire, you will realize that you can probably accomplish anything that you have previously set out to do because now you have built the discipline and healthy self-confidence in your own ability to get through the toughest of goals.

I wish to reiterate: in the introduction, I told you that being a salesperson is not hard; shoveling asphalt is hard. This is true, but the mental stress of getting past the middle of the pack all the way to the top is very difficult. I do not want to make light of it. There is a reason why I put these words in the last chapter, because you had to get past your self-doubt to realize that we have all been there. All successful salespeople constantly battle the inner mind fight. We constantly battle whether we are good enough to get through a difficult task. We have simply realized that it is only imaginary. The negative thoughts in our heads are often not reality. We never have to hop on the train of negative thought.

Your Inner Belief

When it comes to visualizing things, at first it may seem uncomfortable. It may even seem silly to close your eyes and see yourself as a successful person, but it is a very important technique to learn because this is where the process begins. It starts with your inner belief. It begins with believing that you can climb from the middle of the pack to the top. And that you can stay there.

The doubt will always be there. Fear is necessary, as we have learned, but getting past it is possible. Not only is it possible, it is necessary. It may be the hardest thing that you ever do, but once you cross it, you will realize it was not physically hard. It was a lot of strenuous mental work that had to be done to cross the bridge of fire.

You must work on it every single day and you cannot allow the thought of defeat to win. You cannot succumb to the idea that you aren't good enough to win. You cannot dwell on the fact that you have never done this before. Get confident. Get strong in your belief and keep moving forward. Do the things you've read about in this book and do not stop.

It is true that the greatest pain comes from being close and giving up. Follow through. Get there. Learn it. Be confident. Rid yourself of your ego. Recognize your ability to go the distance.

Winners vs. Losers

The difference between winners and losers is winners never quit. As cliché as it might sound, if you quit, you lose. If you keep going and keep doing the things that are proven to work, success will come in time. It is the most magical occurrence of events that I have ever witnessed in my life. Once you set your mind to do something and stop considering the reasons it cannot be done, all the reasons that you can do it begin to show up. Miraculously, the universe coordinates all the elements to help get you there.

It does take commitment. You must be certain that you have made the decision to cut off any possibility of you not getting there. Be ready to burn your boats, face your greatest enemy, and commit to winning. Let go of your excuses and become victorious.

And most importantly, it takes a willingness to help other people. Once you get to the top, you are likely going to have a burning desire and responsibility to help others.

Therefore, I am helping you. I have developed courses to help people get over the bridge of fire. These courses will go over the techniques that are discussed in this book: methodical ways that help with the mindset, how to be honest, how to keep moving forward, how to get through the fear, how to measure activity, and how to win consistently.

The reason why this chapter is named "Get a Jacket" is because it is cold and lonely at the top. You will move past your friends that are middle packers. You will pass those who are not chasing the same goal and they may resent you for it. It will be tough. It is cold and lonely at the top because the people who do not know how to get there – or worse, are unwilling to put in the work to get there – will do everything they can to keep you from reaching the summit.

I was once told that boiling crabs do not need a lid because as soon as one crab starts to crawl out of the pot, the other crabs pull it back into the boiling water. You do not want to fall victim to this. You want to make sure your focus is set on your goal. And once you are locked into that goal, be prepared to do everything you can to get to it. You may have to fight, kicking and screaming, to get away from the middle of the pack.

People will tell you that you are working too hard or too much. That is the enemy of success. People are going to tell you that you are too stressed, and that you should be satisfied with where you are. That is the enemy of success.

Mediocrity is a land where all middle packers congregate and complain about people at the top. You have to get away from that place. You want to be at the top, and then you can help others get there. In doing so, you can help your company be at the top.

You want to be a winner on a winning team. You want to be a contributor to a winning organization. You must decide to stop being mediocre. Mediocre is for the middle-of-the-pack people. These people are not going to want to see you succeed. They are going to tell you that you are not good enough. They are going to tell you the things that you are doing are a waste of time. Do not listen to them. That's their own fear talking. That is their own self-doubt you are hearing. You cannot believe them. You cannot follow their lead. You must tune them out because they do not know how to get to the top. You can help them after you get there, but do not try to force them to take the journey with you when you are getting started.

The worst thing you can do is try to help somebody who does not want help, especially if they try to hold you back while you are on your journey.

You must keep your goals in the front of your mind, mentally strong, and laser-focused. Visualize your success, feel it, maybe even obsess over it. Breathe deeply into your success and do not let others take that away from you.

Common sense is not that common, and you have worked hard to build the knowledge that you now possess. You will have to stop wasting time with people who do not share the same mindset as you.

There are many lessons that are going to be learned from getting from the middle of the pack to the top. Many we have gone over in the last chapter, which is getting past your ego, remembering to be humble and hungry.

One of the benefits of getting to the top is you become a bit of a pachyderm, or thick-skinned. You build the scar tissue it takes to be resilient through tough times. This is something that should not be taken lightly, because you will be able to identify other people's excuses or fear and see it for what it is. You will be able to empathetically understand that it's self-doubt parading as the truth. When you help somebody move through their excuses, move away from the fear, and over the bridge of fire, you are now teaching them to get past their own delusions. Remember when we once told ourselves that we couldn't, we were essentially saying, "I haven't tried everything that it takes to succeed. I have just tried up until I quit."

We essentially said, "I surrender to my excuses. I surrender to my own lies." Now that you've learned how to get past it, you no longer surrender to that. You look at things as opportunities now instead of reasons why you cannot.

As soon as the excuses begin to arise, you recognize that these are not a part of your mentality anymore. Your mindset has simply changed from "I cannot" to "How can I?"

I want to return to the fact that you may have to lose some of your old friends, and that's going to be a tough thing. You do not necessarily need to have the conversation with them, but you will start to promote yourself out of your old friend-group. Some will understand, some will not; it's not your duty to get them to understand your journey if they are unwilling to contribute. It is not your duty or responsibility to force those who do not want to go over their own bridges of fire. The worst thing you can do is continue to invest in a losing bet or a poor investment. And that is somebody who does not want to change, does not want to adjust, has the know-it-all mentality, the "I've tried everything" mentality. Do your best to help but move on when it gets in the way of your success. Do not let the crab pull you back into the boiling pot.

You will gain new friends. You will gain friends that have the same mindset as you. And that mindset is going to carry you a long way. Success begets success.

Once you identify clues and pursue progress, you will begin to see other ways to become successful. You will want to help those who want to help themselves.

You have crossed your own bridge of fire, so be proud. Go and celebrate and keep on winning! You deserve it.

BONUS MATERIALS

BE YOUR BEST

If I were to calculate from my door-to-door days to high-level executive meetings in my 25 years of sales, I have experienced over 60,000 sales interactions. I have witnessed some amazing things and not-so-amazing things. I have put together these bonus materials and will discuss them further in the courses I have developed to make sure you show up being on your best behavior and much more.

Here we will cover the following:

- Posture
- Meeting manners
- Mirroring
- The follow-up
- Using a team correctly
- Questions and clarifying
- Closing and asking for the business
- Five LinkedIn message templates

Posture

Some studies correlate posture with a higher confidence level. It's also suggested that having a better posture will reduce stress hormones too. All in all, having good posture when you are in a face-to-face situation with your customers promotes a healthy self-image on the exterior and interior.

While having good posture is not the only answer for self-esteem issues, it's certainly not a bad place to start. Doing some daily stretches and exercising every day can help promote better posture while sitting or standing.

Right before you enter the meeting, take a deep breath and exhale through your mouth. (If you are alone and no one can hear you, make an "ahh" sound.) When doing this, your tension is released in shoulders and jaw. Being tense is noticeable and obvious and can make you look rigid or aggressive.

When you greet someone, be sure to make eye contact. When approaching for a handshake, extend your hand out with your shoulders back. This confirms that you are friendly and happy to be there, but mean business too.

During the meeting, pay attention to your posture. Do not slouch in the chair; it is not your living room nor are you in front of the TV.

Show confidence with body language. I have taken the time to list out a few. Try and be cognizant of your overall motions but not distracted from the meeting.

Keep your hands out of your pockets. Having your hands out and making slight gestures demonstrates that you are in control of yourself and your content. Keep your hands out of your mouth too. Nail biting is a no-no, in case you have this habit.

Speaking of nails, this is not specifically in the category of posture, but make sure that you are properly groomed. Your hands, face, hair, and clothing can all make or break your appearance. Take time and make sure that you are looking professional and therefore feeling professional and ready to win.

Make sure that you are sitting up straight and leaning forward, elbows on the table with your hands held. Have least one shoulder pointing in towards the customer, preferably with your right ear listening. The right ear is better at receiving speech and helps with the critical thinking portion of the brain. That is the one that you want to use inside of meetings. So not only are you striking the appearance that you are interested, but your brain is working better for you.

Lastly, genuinely smile. The best thing you can do for your posture and promote a healthy self-image is to smile. It is warm and inviting and reduces tension on both sides of the table.

Meeting Manners

Meetings are the most important thing you can use as a tool of leverage for understanding your customers' reactions, their body language, their tone, their pace, their tempo – all of the good stuff needed for conversation flow. More importantly, this helps you understand if you are making an impact. But do not think that the observation is only going one way. Your customers are watching you, and paying attention to everything that you do and say as well.

Making sure that you have meeting manners is critical to ongoing success. It will help promote the relationship and ensure you are welcomed back.

Be on time. Early is the new on time, so make every effort to be there 10 minutes before and plan to do it. You are not so lucky to get the perfect parking every time or avoid a delay. Plan to be early every time without exception.

Do not fidget. Fidgeting is a clear sign of nervousness. Anxiety is often accompanied by restlessness or fidgeting. Jittery legs and bouncing knees are all signs that you are not calm. Pay attention to these and if you begin them, take a deep breath and try and make eye contact. This will remind you that you are in a meeting and your focus and attention needs to be on the customer.

I'm going the list out a few important things that are not so comfortable to discuss, but are **must nots** and need to be strictly adhered to when in meetings. These may seem like common sense but you'll be surprised what I've seen in the thousands of meetings I have been in. There are no exceptions to any of the following and in no such matter should you even consider making an exception. If you disagree, then go back to Chapter 3 and re-read it.

- Never bring up religion or politics. Nobody cares about your views. If you are using it as a way to bond, do not. There are thousands of other things to bond over outside of your personal views on religion and politics so never bring it up – not in a meeting room, not at a happy hour, not at a dinner, not at a breakfast. It's off limits.

- Never do anything that is even remotely close to having any type of racial remarks. Do not talk about other countries or cultures, not even your own. If a customer brings up something about their own culture that is considered controversial, do not add to the comment or conversation.

- Never on any level, any shape, any form, or through any type of innuendos bring up sex. I cannot stress how incredibly inappropriate and ill-mannered it is to bring up anything remotely close to sex – no suggestions around sex, sexual behavior, bedroom talk, or any of it. All of that is off limits and uncouth.

- Never over-talk anybody. Never talk louder or faster when somebody else starts to talk just so you can get your point across. It's rude and disrespectful and it will show them that you are trying to bully them around. Stop talking if someone else begins. Wait your turn, then speak calmly.

Mirroring

Short story is that a long time ago, some Italians stumbled across a study of monkeys in a lab that experienced neurons firing when the opposite mirrored their behavior.

As adults, we do it when we are talking with someone we like, are interested in, or agree with. We subconsciously switch our body posture to match that of the other person – mirroring that person's nonverbal behavior to signal that we are connected and engaged.

The neuroscience behind this "limbic synchrony" has everything to do with the discovery of these "mirror neurons" and how empathy develops in the brain. In human beings, it was found that mirror neurons not only simulate actions, they also reflect intentions and feelings.

Adopting the same gestures, posture, or tone can enhance bonding and help with networking or negotiating—but be subtle about it. Mirroring a conversation partner's gestures, expressions, posture, vocal pitch, or tone can reflect rapport or a desire to please, research shows.

It is seen most often between romantic partners, but it also happens at work in networking sessions, meetings, and conversations with colleagues.

People who are deeply engaged in conversation are often surprised to realize they're mirroring each other. Deliberately trying to mirror another person's behavior without being truly engaged can backfire, however.

Start off subtle and make eye contact. Envision the person you are talking to as the most interesting person on the planet.

Slowly nod three or four times and adopt their posture and facial movement. It may seem silly but it works.

Retail salespeople who were told to mimic the nonverbal and verbal behavior of customers sold more products and left customers with a more positive opinion of the store, according to a 2011 study of 129 customers by French researchers.

In another study, published in 2008 in the *Journal of Experimental Social Psychology*, 62 students were assigned to negotiate with other students. Those who mirrored others' posture and speech reached a settlement 67% of the time, while those who didn't reached a settlement 12.5% of the time.

The Follow-Up

After each interaction, you should have an appropriate type of follow-up. The follow-up will outline what was discussed during your time together, actions, next meeting agenda, and perhaps a little bit of a personal touch to give the impression that you were paying attention. If somebody mentions an album, a restaurant, a book, etc., put that in the follow-up.

A good way of knowing whether or not these types of follow-ups work is to mention them during your next time together. If you are sending follow-ups that are not getting responses, make sure you are tweaking them, adjusting or asking your customer for feedback. Determine if they were able to read it. Another very important thing is to ask them whether or not a follow-up is necessary.

Most managers will make a salesperson write some form of follow-up, but it's very important to determine if these follow-ups are important to your customers.

Ask them and ask them again because one day they may say no, but the next day they may say yes. I do believe follow-ups are extremely courteous and demonstrate a disciplined salesperson.

The follow-up should be succinct and actionable and lead to a second meeting or transaction.

Let's look at an example of a follow-up below.

Follow-Up Example

Subject: Meeting Follow-up

Team,

I do appreciate the time we spent together and your increased interest in the *Bridge of Fire* sales training. I booked a reservation at the Italian place Charlie was raving about and will let you know what I think. I have recapped our discussion below along with assigned actions. My goal is to swiftly move to next steps as discussed in our meeting.

Objective

Acme.com is looking to *Bridge of Fire* to train the newly-hired field sales force. Acme is going through hyper-growth and needing to have a more formal sales training program.

Actions

- *Bridge of Fire* to provide proposal on a weekend course + materials for the 35 newly-hired field sales force.
- Charlie to send over company purchase agreement ahead of time for review.
- Committee to meet and discuss proposal and pricing.

- *Bridge of Fire* to follow up the week after next for signed agreement and start dates.

Please let me know if this accurately captures our discussion, actions, and next steps. Please clarify or add where you see fit. I look forward to working with you all should you choose our organization.

Regards, [Your Name]

Clarifying Questions and Transparency

Do not ask a question and then suggest and answer to your own question. It is rude, and more importantly, when you are talking, your customer is not. Do not make your questions long and drawn out with five or six sentences:

> Hi, I wanted to ask you about your initiatives to see what your initiatives are, because are your initiatives the same as my other customer that has these initiatives? Because I know whenever these people have these types of initiatives, they're going to be doing this with your initiatives. What are your initiatives? I was just wondering what your initiatives were because blah, blah, blah, blah, blah.

It's all about crystal clear communication upfront — being understanding and extremely transparent. Ask for transparency and very specific questions.

Upon asking a question, make sure it is short, succinct, and to the point. If you do not get what you want, follow that up with a question. Do not ask more than three questions in a row. Allow some conversation to take place between question and answer. If at any given time, you feel your customer is uncomfortable, take a step back. Make sure you are prefacing why you are asking these questions, what you are attempting to get out of it, and how you need the correct information to get to the correct solution. Ultimately that is what the customers are wanting.

Once again, understand you do not need to disguise yourself as anything other than a salesperson. Throughout the Q and A process, allow them to ask more questions than you. As stated, salespeople do talk a lot. Sometimes many of those questions are misleading.

Far too often there is needless back and forth. When the customer is making revisions, salespeople tend to get increasingly frustrated or pressured by their managers asking where the deal is. All this can be avoided if you take time for pre-facing and proceed to ask a few simple, clarifying questions up front.

The whole point of sales is to sell the product or service. The end goal in sales is to sell stuff. It is not to quote stuff. It's not to provide information. There is certainly a right way and a wrong way to ask questions. Making sure that you are asking clarifying questions upfront, to help aid the sales process, is very important.

I believe it is completely acceptable to let the customer know that you are in sales and it is your job to sell whatever it is you are selling. Whatever product or service that you may have, it is your job, and you would not be doing your job if you were not getting the right product or service to the right customer. Customers need to be reminded of this from time to time.

So you have to go through a series of qualifying questions to see whether or not your product or service matches your customer's needs. To do this upfront in a way that is helping the sales process will benefit you and your customer. This shouldn't be confrontational. It should not be contentious, but if it moves in that direction, take a step back and help your customer understand that you are trying to provide the most amount of benefit and be as accurate as possible.

You will take all the time needed, but you want to be heading in the right direction. And heading in the right direction is being able to qualify what your customer needs upfront so you are not chasing down the wrong stuff.

Using a Team Correctly

The key to winning often is not linked to being more talented or smarter, but being more resourceful. If you're a one-man show, you have the entire world at your fingertips via the internet to help you create success. If you are on a team or in an organization that has resources that aid to your success, you must know how to use them correctly.

The salesperson is quite often called the quarterback of the account, the account manager, the account executive, or a sales associate. He or she is the person that is managing the sales process, the executive to the account, and managing the account in a way to help move customers towards a product or service. This product or service helps solve a customer's need or problem. In order to maintain a high level of efficiency, you must use resources properly and often.

Before we get into delegation, let's talk about how to treat your team members. If these people are your delegates or on your team, you must show them courtesy and respect. You cannot bark orders at them. You cannot yell at them because nobody likes working in a negative environment. They may help you because it is their job, but they won't like doing it. They may only do a sloppy or low-effort job because you are not being as courteous as you should.

This doesn't mean to be a doormat either, or to fake flattery to get them to do as you want. You can quite succinctly tell them the direction that they need to head, clearly provide your expectations, and ask if you have their permission to hold them accountable. Ultimately, you will want to lay the goals out first, determine who is in charge for each portion, discuss with them what the expectations are and which tasks are their portions, and then ask for a time that it could be done. Before is always better, but on time is what you expect.

Check with them throughout the process to make sure that they're doing okay or in any need of your help, but leave them to be professionals. You only must have a difficult conversation if they do not come through for you. Do not check with them countless times before the date that you told them to have things finished because that is annoying.

Being resourceful is using resources to their fullest capability. In order to do this consistently, you must be professional and err on the side of being kind to your resources. Make sure that you are a good team player and they will want to play on your team. The quarterback has to be able to adjust mid-play in order to create the greatest success. If you are able to communicate exactly what is needed from your resources, you will be able to come together and be on the winning team.

Closing and Asking for the Business

We discussed earlier that success should never be a surprise, nor should closing a deal. You will get a blue bird or get lucky. There's really no technique in that, but closing deals takes technique. There is a formula and a science behind it, and put simply, it's doing everything that needs to be done in order for it to generate a sale. It seems pretty easy. But not so much, because very often being a salesperson hungering for the close may lead you to overlook small details like financing, credit approval, field resources, pricing, competition, etc. All these need to be laid out up front.

During your qualifying and clarifying question period, make sure you are lining out everything that could happen that may not allow this deal to go forward, as well as what exactly will make it go forward. Draw this out. Illustrate it. Either get on a whiteboard, or put it into an email or a Visio. Put something in writing that clearly states exactly what the expectations are in order for you to move forward.

Lay that out clearly and when you are getting close to the end of that timeline, make sure you check in with your customer to see if you are all on pace to close the deal.

When the purchase order comes through, you should not be surprised. Yes, there's a lot of time for celebration, but you really shouldn't be shocked if you were checking in throughout and you've laid this out very clearly upfront.

You can do all tips and tricks and go to closing school and do all the gimmicky stuff that other salespeople do. But truthfully, if the customer is going to buy, they're going to buy. If you've done your job and have done it correctly, then they will buy that product or service from you. Get clear answers from your qualifying period and state them clearly, "If we do this, are we going to be able to move forward? Is there anything outside of your control that will prevent this? Is there anybody else that we should be including in order to make this go forward?"

Once you are very clear on exactly what needs to happen, then you can move it to actually happen. The best thing about sales is that you know you're successful when the deal is closed and when you exceed your quota. Those are very easy ways to determine whether or not you are being successful, and what you are doing is working. But you can't just hope that things are going to happen because hope is not a place for you to put trust into. Hoping that you're doing the right things will never gets you the results that you're looking for. Hope + Hope = More Hope. You have to be very, very crystal clear, and even clear with yourself to ask, "Am I doing everything I know that needs to be done in order to make this thing move forward?" Get after it!

Five LinkedIn Message Templates

The Common Group Email

Research the prospect online. Look for mutual interests, hobbies, or acquaintances. You could discover common ground and a reason to reach out.

Approach with caution. You want to come across as having done your homework, not creepy.

"Hi [Prospect Name],

Our mutual connection, [Connection Name], and I were talking recently about [hot topic]. She said you were an expert on this issue.

I'm writing an article about [hot topic] because it's relevant, timely, yet confusing to many of my customers. Can I include your perspective, [Prospect Name]?

Regards, [Your Name]"

The Problem Solver Email

Prospects are looking for guidance and advice on how to tackle a problem. Tailor your email that way to get their attention.

64% of B2B buyers appreciate it when a salesperson contacts them with relevant information. While it's okay to lightly mention your offering as a solution, you might be better off saving that for later.

"Hi [Prospect Name],

Your LinkedIn post discussing how your company is struggling to overcome [problem] made me think of others I know experiencing the same frustration.

Bridge of Fire

What seems to work is when companies tackle these three core issues:

- Lack of integrated systems
- Manual processes
- Unawareness about the latest options

Let me know if you'd like me to send an eBook my company put together that spells out how to address these issues effectively.

Regards, [Your Name]"

The Case Study Email

Use the power of peer influence: highlight a similar company or customer, and show how your solution made a difference. Take note that 67% of B2B buyers rely on peer recommendations and 41% on case studies when making a final purchasing decision. If executed well (and without sounding self-serving), this email can capture attention and trigger a response.

"Hi [Prospect Name],

Your latest company blog post showcases your strategic initiative to do [initiative name]. Congratulations on spearheading such an important endeavor!

As you prepare to move forward, you'll be interested to learn how others in your position pulled off the same project successfully. In fact, I know of [Prospect's role] in three companies very similar to yours that generated an average of 17% higher revenues by using [your solution] to power their new processes.

[Prospect Name], let me know if you'd like me to forward the case studies detailing how they achieved such impressive results.

Regards, [Your Name]"

The Giver Email

Few people will turn down a free offer. Focus on a giveaway, whether it's an eBook, a free trial, or a free evaluation. The more exclusive or insightful the offer, the more valuable it will be perceived by the client.

"Hi [Prospect Name],

Your content-rich website is visually stunning, but I ran a performance test that shows it might not be loading quickly enough for your site visitors.

Would you like to see the results and how your site compares to the competition?

Regards, [Your Name]"

The No-Nonsense Email

Sometimes you need a straightforward message to drive a sale. Write the shortest email possible with bullet points, quickly describing how your solution can benefit the prospect.

"Hi [Prospect Name],

Now that you have trialed [product or service] for three months, I want to confirm you are experiencing the impact we discussed:

- *Less manual data entry*
- *Faster financial closings*
- *More accurate monthly reports*

Bridge of Fire

What are the next steps to get you signed up for an enterprise license, so your entire finance team can take advantage of [product]?

Regards, [Your Name]"

References

[1] Wikipedia Contributors. (2019, December 2). Pareto principle. Retrieved December 17, 2019, from https://en.wikipedia.org/wiki/Pareto_principle

[2] Hedges, Nick. (2015, May 6). *What Separates the Top 20% of Salespeople from the Bottom 80%.* Retrieved from https://www.inc.com/nick-hedges/what-separates-the-top-20-of-salespeople-from-the-bottom-80.html

[3] The Man Who Broke The 4-Minute Mile. (1964, April 18). *The New York Times.* Retrieved from https://www.nytimes.com/1964/04/19/archives/the-man-who-broke-the-4minute-mile.html

[4] Malaysian Exploding Ant: An Explosive Legacy. (n.d.). *Animal Kingdom Defense Mechanisms.* Retrieved from: https://animaldefensemechanisms.weebly.com/malaysian-exploding-ant.html

[5] Winkler, Rolfe. (2015, April 21). Google gives boost to mobile-friendly sites. *The Wall Street Journal.* Retrieved from https://www.wsj.com/articles/google-gives-boost-to-mobile-friendly-sites-1429660022

[6] Long, Weldon. (2019, February 8). Getting Over Your Fear of Cold Calling Customers. *Harvard Business Review.* Retrieved from https://hbr.org/2019/02/getting-over-your-fear-of-cold-calling-customers

[7] Marsh, Abigail. (2013, October 28). The Chemistry of Fear: A new video from the American Chemical Society. *American Chemical Society.* Retrieved from https://www.acs.org/content/acs/en/pressroom/newsreleases/2013/october/the-chemistry-of-fear-a-new-video-from-the-acs.html

[8] Ruiz, Don Miguel. (1997). *The Four Agreements*. San Rafael, California: Amber-Allen Publishing.

[9] Cortés Burns His Boats. (n.d.). *PBS.org*. Retrieved from: https://www.pbs.org/conquistadors/cortes/cortes_d00.html

[10] Wikipedia Contributors. (2019, November 2). God complex. Retrieved December 17, 2019, from https://en.wikipedia.org/wiki/God_complex

Index

Accountability, 26
Adapting, 36
Appreciation, 93
Bad situation, 46
Confidence, 94
Customers
    Measure actual sales, 69
    Sales database, 71
    Sales pitch, 70
Ego
    How to eliminate, 92
    Versus confidence, 94
Fear, 51
    Common fears in salespeople, 52
    Usefulness, 54
FITFO model, 34
Follow-up, 110
Habit

Being trustworthy, 45
Excuses, 28
Going above and beyond, 45
Speaking up, 50
Honesty, 31
Longevity, 32
Manners, 107
Mentor, 24
Mindset, 21
    Mental check, 75
Mirroring, 109
Pareto principle, 17
Posture, 105
Prospect, 63
    Communication, 66
    Identifying, 64
    List, 65, 71
Trust, 41

www.ingramcontent.com/pod-product-compliance
Lightning Source LLC
Chambersburg PA
CBHW032055150426
43194CB00006B/531